WITHDRAWN

HARVARD LIBRARY

WITHDRAWN

AN EXPLORER OF REALMS

OF ART, LIFE, AND THOUGHT

ABOUT THE AUTHOR

Dr. John E. Rexine is Charles A. Dana Professor of the Classics and Chairman of the Classics Department of Colgate University. A graduate of Harvard College in 1951, he received his A.B. degree *magna cum laude* and was elected a member of Phi Beta Kappa. He also received his A.M. (1953) and Ph.D. (1964) degrees from Harvard University, and holds an honorary Doctor of Letters degree from Hellenic College/Greek Orthodox School of Theology (1981). He has been on the Colgate Faculty since 1957, has served as Chairman of the Department of the Classics, Chairman of the Department of Classics, Slavic, and Oriental Languages, Director of the Division of University Studies, Director of the Colgate - IBM Corporation Institute in the Liberal Arts Program for Executives, Director of the Division of the Humanities, Associate Dean of the Faculty, and Acting Dean of the Faculty. Prior to coming to Colgate, he taught at Brandeis University, and in the Fall Term 1972-1973 was Visiting Professor of Greek in the College Year in Athens Program in Greece.

During 1979-1980 Dr. Rexine was a Senior Fulbright Research Scholar in Athens at the Gennadius Library. He has been editor of *The Classical Outlook*, associate editor of *The Greek Orthodox Theological Review*, and book review editor for *Athene, The Modern Language Journal, The Hellenic Chronicle, The Orthodox Observer,* and *The Patristic and Byzantine Review*. He is the author or co-author of several books, numerous articles, and over a thousand book reviews.

Prof. Rexine is a member of a number of archaeological, classical, philological, and theological professional organizations, and is listed in *Who's Who in America* and *Who's Who in the World*.

OTHER BOOKS BY
DR. JOHN E. REXINE

SOLON AND HIS POLITICAL THEORY

RELIGION IN PLATO AND CICERO

AN OUTLINE OF TACITUS

AN OUTLINE OF THUCYDIDES

THE HELLENIC SPIRIT:
BYZANTINE AND POST BYZANTINE

CONSTANTINE CAVARNOS

AN EXPLORER OF REALMS
OF ART, LIFE, AND THOUGHT

A SURVEY OF THE WORKS OF
PHILOSOPHER AND THEOLOGIAN
CONSTANTINE CAVARNOS

By

JOHN E. REXINE, Ph.D., Litt.D.

INSTITUTE FOR BYZANTINE
AND MODERN GREEK STUDIES
115 Gilbert Road
Belmont, Massachusetts 02178
U.S.A.

All rights reserved
Copyright 1985, by John E. Rexine
Published by THE INSTITUTE FOR BYZANTINE
AND MODERN GREEK STUDIES, INC.
115 Gilbert Road, Belmont, Massachusetts 02178, U.S.A.
Library of Congress Catalog Card Number: 85-81278
Printed in the United States of America

Clothbound ISBN 0-914744-69-0
Paperbound ISBN 0-914744-70-4

PREFACE

1985 marks the forty-third year since Dr. Constantine Cavarnos' graduation from Harvard College (A.B., *magna cum laude*) in the field of philosophy. He has been very much a Harvard man, having gone on to receive his Master of Arts and Doctor of Philosophy degrees from Harvard in the same field, and having spent a good deal of his professional and personal life in the Harvard area. But the year 1985 also marks the year of his departure from the United States for permanent residence in Greece. During these four decades, Dr. Cavarnos has taught philosophy at a number of American colleges and universities, founded and directed the Institute for Byzantine and Modern Greek Studies, lectured widely on both sides of the Atlantic, published books, articles, and book reviews, edited and translated publications in philosophy and religion, but more than anything else, brought to the English-speaking world a wealth of Greek Orthodox material hitherto unavailable in English on Orthodox Christian art, life and thought, and on modern Orthodox saints. A lifetime of work has yielded a rich crop that will be available to all for years to come.

It has been my good fortune to have known Dr. Cavarnos for over three decades and to have read virtually all of his published work in Greek and English. It has also turned out that I have been the only person to have had the distinction of having reviewed all thirty-three of his books (i.e., all that have been published to date). It seemed, therefore, only appropriate that this collection of reviews be presented to him at this special time, as he completes a major phase of his professional life and begins another in the country to which he has given so much over the course of his lifetime. We can all be sure that more contributions will be forthcoming that will be worthy of our attention. But, in the meantime, this book will serve as a modest recognition of a lifetime of work *"eis osmen euodias pneumatikes" (as an offering of spiritual fragrance)*.

JOHN E. REXINE

May, 1985
Hamilton, New York

ACKNOWLEDGMENTS

Acknowledgment is made of assistance from the Colgate Research Council and the Colgate Humanities Division Faculty Development Fund in the preparation of this book. The author also wishes his readers to note that occasionally omissions have been made in reprinting the reviews in order to avoid unnecessary repetition; that many corrections and revisions have been made throughout the book; that the chapter headings of the book are *the titles* of Dr. Cavarnos' books; and that thirty-three books are dicussed in as many chapters. The Cavarnos bibliography, though not complete by any means, is the most comprehensive to be found in any single publication published to date and serves to document the range and variety of Cavarnos' publications.

Finally, the author wishes to thank the editors of *Athene, Balkan Studies, Diakonia, The Greek Orthodox Theological Review, The Greek World, The Hellenic Chronicle, The Hellenic Journal, The Hellenic Times, The Newsletter of the Classical Association of the Empire State, The Patristic and Byzantine Review, Speculum,* and *St. Vladimir's Theological Quarterly* for publishing the original versions of his reviews and for the permission to include them in this volume, and Dr. Cavarnos for permission to use the title-pages and many illustrations from his books.

CONTENTS

PREFACE.................................... 7
ACKNOWLEDGMENTS..................... 9
INTRODUCTION........................... 13

PART I
PHILOSOPHICAL WORKS

1. *A DIALOGUE BETWEEN BERGSON, ARISTOTLE, AND PHILOLOGOS*...................... 18
2. *MAN AND THE UNIVERSE IN AMERICAN PHILOSOPHY*................. 23
3. *MODERN GREEK PHILOSOPHERS ON THE HUMAN SOUL*...................... 27
4. *BYZANTINE THOUGHT AND ART*............. 32
5. *MODERN GREEK THOUGHT*................... 40
6. *PLATO'S THEORY OF FINE ART*............... 44
7. *PLATO'S VIEW OF MAN*...................... 47
8. *THE CLASSICAL THEORY OF RELATIONS*...... 51
9. *A DIALOGUE ON G.E. MOORE'S ETHICAL PHILOSOPHY*................... 54
10. *PHILOSOPHICAL STUDIES*................... 58
11. *THE EDUCATIONAL THEORY OF BENJAMIN OF LESVOS*............................... 64

PART II
WORKS ON ORTHODOX CHRISTIAN ART, LIFE, AND THOUGHT

1. *BYZANTINE SACRED MUSIC*.................. 70
2. *BYZANTINE SACRED ART*.................... 73

CONTENTS 11

3. ORTHODOXY IN AMERICA................... 79
4. ANCHORED IN GOD....................... 82
5. THE HOLY MOUNTAIN.................... 88
6. THE CONVENT OF EVANGELISTRIA........... 93
7. SYMBOLS AND PROOFS OF IMMORTALITY..... 95
8. THE QUESTION OF THE UNION OF
    THE TWO CHURCHES.................... 99
9. GREECE AND ORTHODOXY...............102
10. THE ORTHODOX TRADITION AND
    MODERNIZATION........................106
11. GREEK LETTERS AND ORTHODOXY...........109
12. ORTHODOX ICONOGRAPHY.................. 112
13. WAYS AND MEANS TO SANCTITY.............117
14. THE FUTURE LIFE ACCORDING TO
    ORTHODOX TEACHING.................. 121

PART III
MODERN ORTHODOX SAINTS

1. ST. COSMAS AITOLOS...................... 126
2. ST. MACARIOS OF CORINTH.................. 130
3. ST. NICODEMOS THE HAGIORITE.............134
4. ST. NIKEPHOROS OF CHIOS................... 139
5. ST. SERAPHIM OF SAROV..................... 143
6. ST. ARSENIOS OF PAROS..................... 149
7. ST. NECTARIOS OF AEGINA.................. 153
8. ST. SAVVAS THE NEW....................... 158

BIBLIOGRAPHY: WORKS BY CONSTANTINE
    CAVARNOS............................. 163
INDEX..176

INTRODUCTION*

It would be difficult to think of a single individual in America today who has done as much for the promotion of classical philosophy, Byzantine art, and Greek Orthodox ascetical theology as has Constantine Cavarnos, author of thirty-three books and co-author of a number of others, the writer of dozens of articles, reviews and pamphlets, and the translator of a significant number of important works. Born in Boston, Massachusetts, educated at Harvard University, from which he received his A.B., A.M., and Ph.D. degrees, Constantine Cavarnos has taught at Harvard, Tufts, Wellesley, the University of North Carolina at Chapel Hill, Hellenic College/Greek Orthodox School of Theology at Brookline, Wheaton College (Norton, Mass.), and Clark University. He also had the distinction of being Fulbright Research Scholar in Modern Greek Thought at the University of Athens for two academic years (1957-1959). Currently, he is President of the Institute for Byzantine and Modern Greek Studies in Belmont, Massachusetts, an organization founded in 1956 to study Byzantine and Modern Greek art, thought, language, and culture in general; to make this knowledge accessible to scholars and the general public; and to show the value of Byzantine and Modern Greek civilization to present day American life and culture through research,

---

*Published under the title "Dr. Constantine Cavarnos: A Man Anchored in God," in *The Greek World*, Vol. 2, Nos. 5-6, Sept.-Dec. 1977, p. 40.

friendly discussions, public lectures, symposia, and publications. Dr. Cavarnos, a quiet, gentle, and prayerful man, has devoted his entire life to the fulfillment of these goals as professor, lecturer, scholar, author, and publisher.

In the area of systematic philosophy Dr. Cavarnos has been interested in ethics, aesthetics, logic, metaphysics, problems of philosophy, and philosophy of religion. In the area of history of philosophy he has concerned himself with the Pre-Socratic philosophers, Plato and Aristotle, mediaeval philosophy, modern European philosophy, modern Greek philosophy, and American philosophy. But beyond this, he is probably best known for his work in Byzantine art and music, Orthodox hagiography, ascetical theology, and modern Greek thought in all its manifestations.

In the field of philosophy, he has published such original works as *A Dialogue between Bergson, Aristotle, and Philologos* (1949, 1973); *Man and the Universe in American Philosophy* (1959); *Modern Greek Philosophers on the Human Soul* (1967); *Byzantine Thought and Art* (1968, 1974, 1980); *Modern Greek Thought* (1969); *Plato's Theory of Fine Art* (1973); *Plato's View of Man* (1975, 1982); *The Classical Theory of Relations* (1975); *A Dialogue on G.E. Moore's Ethical Philosophy* (1979); *Philosophical Studies* (1979); and *The Educational Theory of Benjamin of Lesvos* (1984). These works show clearly a competence and concern ranging from the psychology and the aesthetics of Plato and the category of relation in Plato, Aristotle and Thomism to the metaphysics, epistemology, philosophy of religion, ethics, political theory and aesthetics of American and European philosophers. They also show perceptive analyses of Byzantine philosophical and theological thought, as well as of the arts of Byzantium, particularly iconog-

INTRODUCTION 15

raphy, hymnody and music. And they introduce to the contemporary reader otherwise little known modern Greek thinkers, from the middle of the 18th century to the present, on the fine arts, science, the nature and destiny of man, and philosophy of education.

In the area of theology and religion, Dr. Cavarnos has contributed in Greek or English such remarkable works as *Byzantine Sacred Music* (1956, 1966, 1974, 1981); *Byzantine Sacred Art* (1957, 1985), *Orthodoxy in America* (1958); *Anchored in God* (1959, 1975); *Symbols and Proofs of Immortality* (1964); *The Question of Union* (1964, 1968); *Greece and Orthodoxy* (1967); *The Convent of Evangelistria of Plomarion, Lesvos* (1970); *The Orthodox Tradition and Modernization* (1971); *The Holy Mountain* (1973, 1977); *Greek Letters and Orthodoxy* (1976); *Orthodox Iconography* (1977, 1980); and an unusually valuable series on *Modern Orthodox Saints* that has thus far included *St. Cosmas Aitolos* (1971, 1975, 1985), *St. Macarios of Corinth* (1972, 1977), *St. Nicodemos the Hagiorite* (1974, 1979), *St. Nikephoros of Chios* (1976, 1985), *St. Arsenios of Paros* (1978), *St. Seraphim of Sarov* (1980, 1984), *St. Nectarios of Aegina* (1981), and *St. Savvas the New* (1985).

In all the work that Dr. Cavarnos has produced — and continues to produce — he returns to the sources, whether they be classical, mediaeval, or modern. And he confronts the reader directly with those sources, with frequent comparisons between Eastern and Western modes of expression, always with penetrating, in-depth exposition, analysis and explanation of the material, in lucid language and style that can be appreciated by layman and scholar alike.

A frequent visitor to Greece and his parents' island of Lesvos, a forthright proponent and expositor of the finest and most profound aspects of the Greek Orthodox heritage, a severe critic of superficial Hellenism and surface Orthodoxy, Constantine Cavarnos, a man of God and a true son of Hellas and America, is himself truly "anchored in God" and through his work has enriched the lives of all the contemporary bearers and heirs of the Hellenic and Byzantine traditions.

PART I

PHILOSOPHICAL WORKS

A DIALOGUE

BETWEEN

Bergson, Aristotle and Philologos

By

Constantine Cavarnos, Ph. D.

CAMBRIDGE, MASSACHUSETTS

1949

1
A DIALOGUE BETWEEN BERGSON, ARISTOTLE, AND PHILOLOGOS*

Originally printed in 1949, *A Dialogue between Bergson, Aristotle, and Philologos* was the winner of a prestigious Bowdoin Prize at Harvard University in 1947, and constitutes Constantine Cavarnos' "first book." It is his first philosophical dialogue, in which the basic and dominant questions are, according to Harvard Professor John Wild in the Preface: (1) "What is that ever present dynamism and change with which the whole world of nature is always pulsating?" (2) "What is that rational insight or awareness which is the peculiar possession of man?"

In this lively interchange of ideas, Bergson is very much the center of attention or, at least, argument. Bergson is represented as one whose interest in philosophy is purely theoretical, and not at all concerned with action or utility, who insists that reality can be known by intuition – intuition which apprehends the external world or matter ("pure perception"), and intuition which apprehends the internal world or spirit ("pure memory"). In the perception of external objects *"we grasp . . . at one and the same time, a 'state' of our consciousness and a 'reality' independent of ourselves.* This mixed character of our immediate percep-

---

*Review published in *The Hellenic Times*, October 2, 1980, under the title: "Skillful Use of dramatic Dialogue Introduces the Reader to Two of the Western World's Greatest Philosophical Figures."

tion, this appearance of a realized contradiction is the principal theoretical reason that we have for believing in *an external world which does not coincide absolutely with our perception.*" In this dialogue, Aristotle criticizes Bergson's view of perception as very subjectivistic, and reacts strongly to Bergson's statement that matter is *"the aggregate of images, and 'perception of matter' these same images referred to the eventual action of one particular image, my body"* (p. 28). He points out an abandonment of the distinction between mind and matter and reduction of everything to mind and the mental, either conscious or unconscious, and accuses Bergson of idealism (the word is used here to mean mentalism) in the name of common sense. Bergson counters by insisting that reality is fundamentally spiritual or mental: "Spirit is the movement of reality upward, matter is the movement of reality downward. Spirit is the tension of reality, the inextensive, heterogeneous movement which creates itself; it is the primal *vital impetus* itself. Matter, on the other hand, is the extension of the detension of the tension of life ...." (p. 30).

Instead of perception, Bergson prefers the word "intuition" — that is, "instinct that has become disinterested and self-conscious, capable of reflecting upon its object and of enlarging it indefinitely" (p. 31.). Philologos gets concerned over Bergson's use of intuition as instinct capable of reflecting, intellectual as against non-intellectual, and is troubled that Bergson's "intuition" makes the senses theoretically and actually superfluous. In order to clarify his position, Bergson sets out to discuss the intuition of spirit ("pure memory") which he finds similar to the intuition of matter, "in that by it one enters into the object, entirely overcomes externality and coincides with the object, dispensing entirely with concepts" (p. 35).

Philologos points out that pure memory involves a multiplicity of qualities; and Aristotle, that until the intellect has performed an act of abstraction ("the drawing out of the

HENRI BERGSON

universal") upon sense perception and memory there can be no knowledge, and that the universal is *in* experience. Bergson's point is that the intellect is incapable of grasping change – physical or psychical ("Reality is nothing but change") (p. 40).

Philologos next takes issue with Bergson's view of the intellect as not at all a theoretical faculty, but one concerned with acting and producing or making. He tries to show that Bergson confuses theoretical with practical reason, depending too heavily on Kant's *Critique of Pure Reason* as definitive with regard to reason, and echoing Kant in what he says about the intellect and intellectual knowledge.

Later on, Bergson says that "reality itself, in the profoundest meaning of the word, is reached by the combined and progressive development of 'science,' which employs the intellect, and 'philosophy,' which employs intuition. Science is *indispensable* to philosophy" (p. 51). Aristotle sees in Bergson's use of intuition his own use of *induction*, at one point. Bergson's "spirit of analysis" Aristotle calls *abstraction;* Bergson's "spirit of synthesis" he calls "the comparison of the form with other perfectly similar forms, seeing that the concept applies equally well to all" (p. 55). Aristotle insists upon structure being in reality and, with Philologos, believes that Bergson's theory of knowledge needs to be considerably modified to be persuasive. Bergson's epistemology is held to be vitiated by a defective metaphysics, which subjectivizes structure.

In this publication, Dr. Cavarnos has skillfully used the dramatic dialogue to present us with the problems of change, knowledge, and the structure of reality by introducing us to two of the Western world's greatest philosophical figures.

2

MAN AND THE UNIVERSE, IN AMERICAN PHILOSOPHY*

Prof. Cavarnos' *Man and the Universe in American Philosophy (To Sympan kai ho Anthropos sten Amerikanike Philosophia)* is written in lucid modern Greek. This book has a particular distinction, because it is to date the only book in Greek devoted entirely to American philosophy, and as such performs a distinct contribution to the cultural exchange program between the United States and Greece under the Fulbright Act. The book is based primarily on three lectures delivered by Dr. Cavarnos in Greece during his second year of tenure as a Research Professor at the University of Athens (1957-1959), plus a supplementary chapter on recent philosophical trends in America.

The first three chapters deal primarily with Ralph Waldo Emerson (1803-1882), William James (1842-1910), and Alfred North Whitehead (1861-1947). These three distinguished philosophers are chosen by Dr. Cavarnos because they reflect three successive periods in American philosophy, and for him these men are the most important and most representative of American philosophers. Incidental discussion of other notable figures in American thought is included.

---

*Review published in *The Hellenic Chronicle*, December 31, 1959.

Κωνσταντίνου Καβαρνοῦ

ΤΟ ΣΥΜΠΑΝ
ΚΑΙ
Ο ΑΝΘΡΩΠΟΣ
ΣΤΗΝ ΑΜΕΡΙΚΑΝΙΚΗ ΦΙΛΟΣΟΦΙΑ

Μαζὶ μὲ ἕνα δοκίμιο γιὰ τὶς σύγχρονες φιλοσοφικὲς τάσεις στὴν Ἀμερική

ΕΚΔΟΤΙΚΟΣ ΟΙΚΟΣ «ΑΣΤΗΡ»
ΑΛ. & Ε. ΠΑΠΑΔΗΜΗΤΡΙΟΥ
ΛΥΚΟΥΡΓΟΥ 10 — ΑΘΗΝΑΙ — 1959

ΟΥ·Ι·ΛΛΙΑΜ ΤΖΑΙΗΜΣ
(WILLIAM JAMES)

In the final chapter, "Contemporary Philosophical Trends in America," discussion of the relations of philosophical studies to classical and Byzantine scholarship in this country is also made.

The topic "Man and the Universe" was chosen because, in Dr. Cavarnos' opinion, all other philosophical topics are subsidiary to or dependent upon these two, and consequently a discussion of American philosophy from this point of view will enable the reader to see the most fundamental theses of each thinker's philosophy.

Handsomely produced, *Man and the Universe in American Philosophy* is an excellent introductory account of the three philosophical giants of American thought and a handy analysis of recent trends in American philosophy.

3

MODERN GREEK PHILOSOPHERS ON THE HUMAN SOUL*

The relevance of the ancient Greek tradition and Byzantine Christian Orthodoxy to modern Greek thought is revealed in this book, in which for the first time in English a serious attempt is made to present the reader with a representative view of some key modern Greek thinkers on a topic that used to be of primary importance to ancient philosophers and medieval theologians, and which is still important to a people who are predominantly Orthodox Christian in religion. What Dr. Cavarnos had done in 1959 in his book *Man and the Universe in American Philosophy* for Greek readers, that is, presenting a representative and concise view of American philosophy and philosophers, he now does for English readers, only this time presenting Greek thinkers in their own words in translation on a specific theme. Again, the importance of the subject is one that relates directly to Professor Cavarnos' Christian concern, though a careful reading of the excerpts will indicate that the arguments proferred for the immortality of the human soul are not necessarily Christian (cf. J. E. Rexine, *Religion in Plato and Cicero,* New York, 1959, pp. 26-30, 34-37).

This book is closely related to Cavarnos' *Symbols and Proofs of Immortality* (Athens, 1964), written in Greek, and should be used in conjunction with it. The mode of pre-

---

*Review published in *Diakonia,* Vol. 5; No. 1, 1970, pp. 62-63.

MODERN GREEK PHILOSOPHERS ON THE HUMAN SOUL

Selections from the writings of Five Representative Thinkers of Modern Greece on the Nature and Immortality of the Soul, translated and edited with a Preface, Introduction, and Notes

By

CONSTANTINE CAVARNOS

INSTITUTE FOR BYZANTINE
AND MODERN GREEK STUDIES
115 Gilbert Road
Belmont, Massachusetts

sentation of material is similar to that employed in *Byzantine Sacred Art* (New York, 1957), in which selections from the iconographer Fotis Kontoglou are made to represent the artist on Byzantine art. So here, five men, whose works as represented in this volume range in date from 1820 to 1949, speak for themselves, and are introduced by brief biographical notes, translated in selections from their works, explained where necessary in footnotes by Cavarnos and compared with other philosophers where appropriate. A bibliographical note on additional reading suggests that the topic has by no means been exhausted.

The authors included are Benjamin of Lesvos (1762-1824) on the existence of the soul as a spiritual substance, freedom of the soul, and immortality of the soul; Petros Vrailas-Armenis (1812-1884) on the nature of the soul, and science and the soul; Ioannis Skaltsounis (1824-1905) on criticism of materialism, and on the spiritual nature of the soul and its immortality; St. Nectarios Kephalas (1846-1920) on prolegomena and proofs of the soul's immortality; and Ioannis Theodorakopoulos (1900-1981) on the nature of the soul and immortality, and on man's faith.

Dr. Cavarnos feels that the subject dealt with by these five modern Greek thinkers has been neglected in our time and needs careful study. Perhaps one could do no better than to cite the late Prof. Theodorakopoulos' final sentences which close the textual portion of the book. "Our epoch," he says, "is more remote than all others from the Socratic standpoint, (which reversed the movement of knowledge from outward inward). That man comes first, that his inner spiritual hypostasis is what should be of infinite concern to each man, this our epoch seems to have entirely forgotten. Today, general schemas and constructs stifle the concrete man, the unique and intrinsic value

Ioannis Theodorakopoulos

called man. Now in order to pay attention to the root of one's self and see one's being as an eternal point, which no general schema can interpret and no theory can vindicate, one requires not only self-concentration, but also faith. Through faith there opens up an infinite concern about the absolute value of personality. Faith has this special characteristic, that it develops an infinite concern about the value of the soul. Faith, however, is a leap beyond mere knowledge, is a self-affirmation of the value called *man* that relates man to eternity."

The reader will find certain of the statements and arguments in this book dated, and will probably be most impressed with the thoughtful comments of the most recent figure represented, Ioannis Theodorakopoulos, who speaks in a language that is contemporary. But the serious student of modern Greek thought and of Orthodox thought should ponder long what is presented here and think carefully of its relation to Eastern Christianity. Professor Cavarnos, by bringing this material to a wider, English-reading audience, has done pioneering work in an area in which practically nothing is known outside of Greece.

BYZANTINE THOUGHT AND ART

A COLLECTION OF ESSAYS

BY

CONSTANTINE CAVARNOS

INSTITUTE FOR BYZANTINE
AND MODERN GREEK STUDIES
115 Gilbert Road
Belmont, Massachusetts

4

BYZANTINE THOUGHT AND ART*

One scholar has described Constantine Cavarnos as the most knowledgeable person in the field of Greek Orthodox ascetical theology in America today. Dr. Cavarnos would probably modestly reject any such claim. Trained as a student of philosophy, with the A.B., A.M., and Ph.D. degrees with distinction from Harvard University, he has taught philosophy at Harvard, the University of North Carolina, the Greek Orthodox School of Theology, Wheaton College, and Clark University, and has been a Fulbright Research Scholar in Modern Greek Thought at the University of Athens. Professor Cavarnos would, I suspect, look upon himself as a serious student of Eastern Orthodox thought, an aesthetician of Byzantine art, and a humble servant of God. Unlike many philosophers of our time, his study of philosophy has led him to a deeper commitment to Christianity. As an author, he writes simply, lucidly, and penetratingly. He does this in both English and modern Greek. Never is he interested in overwhelming his readers with the weight of his scholarly appurtenances, but always in offering them well researched, clearly presented material that has a direct bearing on their lives as Christians, and particularly on their lives as heirs of the Byzantine Orthodox Christian tradition.

---

*Review published in *Diakonia*, Vol. 3, No. 4, 1968, pp. 451-453.

His handsomely produced volume *Byzantine Thought and Art* is ample testimony to his work as a Christian scholar and teacher. The ten essays in this tome, seven of which have been previously published in journals or books, are an accurate indicator of his principal interests, namely, in the fields of Byzantine art and music, philosophy, and theology. It is most valuable and useful to have these essays gathered together in a single book. Even though they were written at different times and for a variety of audiences and purposes, the essays give the work a remarkable coherence as a book. It is well worth pointing out that we now have an abundance of publications on Byzantine history, civilization, and even art in various languages, including English, from an historical viewpoint, but Professor Cavarnos' distinct contribution is to interpret Byzantine philosophy, theology, art and music in their deeper essence and significance as manifestations and expressions of Orthodox Christian religiosity. He shows clearly and unequivocally how far astray one can go when one interprets Byzantine art, philosophy, music or even theology as mere academic subjects, devoid of religious commitment. For example, in the case of philosophy the Byzantines viewed religious faith as indispensable: "The philosopher must begin with religious faith, if he is to avoid error and attain truth" (p. 30). According to the Greek Fathers, "Christianity is the truest and highest philosophy *(philosophia),* because it was revealed by Christ, Who is God's Wisdom *(Sophia)"* (p. 17). In the case of Byzantine art, he rightly emphasizes that for the Byzantines, as for modern Orthodox Christians, "these sacred art objects have an additional value, far more important than aesthetic experience. This value resides in the effects these objects have upon the moral and spiritual nature

9. The Holy Virgin Mary and the Child Christ. Panel icon. 1961. By Fotis Kontoglou and his pupil Constantine Georgakopoulos.

of those who contemplate them. The Church building and the icon are regarded not merely as objects that delight us, but rather as vivid reminders of a reality beyond themselves, of things transcendent, supernatural, and as potent aids for our inner purification and transformation. The important thing about a church for the Byzantines is the fact that its form and beauty are such that they remind us of Heaven, of God, and of the soul as a temple of God to be made pure and to be adorned with every virtue. Similarly, the important thing about icons is that they cause us to recall the sacred persons and events depicted, and the truths of Christian religion, thereby arousing our moral and spiritual zeal, and reinforcing our efforts to imitate the sacred persons and live in the light of religious truth" (p. 72). So, too, in the case of Byzantine music, music appreciation or artistic display is not the primary or even motivating factor. The aim of Byzantine sacred music is, in the first place, to serve as "a means of worship and veneration; and in the second place, as a means of self-perfection, of eliciting and cultivating man's higher thoughts and feelings, and of opposing and eliminating his lower, undesirable ones" (p. 97).

So, throughout the ten essays, Dr. Cavarnos endeavors to illuminate the nature and purpose of the Byzantine heritage and what it means in terms of the Orthodox Church and the Orthodox Christian. In his essays on "Philosophy;" "The Way to Knowledge;" "Conscience;" "The *Philokalia;*" "Aesthetic Examination of Byzantine Art;" "Iconography;" "Manuel Panselinos;" "El Greco and Byzantine Painting;" "Sacred Music;" and "Hymnody," together with the valuable notes, glossary, and index at the end of the book, Professor Cavarnos has given the reader not only a compendium of useful information on Byzantine thought and art, in which frequent comparisons are made between Western and Eastern modes of expression, but also a penetrating, in-depth exposition, analysis and explaation of the religious nature of the Byzantine tradition, backed up by a perceptive reading in the original sources themselves. *Byzantine Thought and Art* is an indispensable guide for anyone claiming interest in Byzantium or the Greek Orthodox Church.

Another Look at the Book*

There is no doubt that within recent years there has been considerable attention paid to the mediaeval Greek world and that a great many works in all of the major languages have been published dealing with Byzantine history, art, and civilization. Still, there are some areas of the Byzantine experience that need further probing, and this is particularly true of what might be described as the subject of the Byzantine mind, especially as it relates to Byzantine religiosity. Dr. Cavarnos, trained as a philosopher and especially interested in aesthetics, but also deeply versed in patristics and ascetical theology, is particularly well qualified to delve more deeply in the philosophical and theological significance of the Byzantine achievement, and is quick to guide the reader to the heart of the Byzantine position. It is no wonder that the author, whose special interests include Byzantine art and music, as well as

---
*Review published in *Speculum,* Vol. XLV, No. 1, January 1970, pp. 118-119. The review has been abridged somewhat in order to avoid as much as possible repeating what has been said in the previous one.

philosophy and theology, should be interested in bringing together within one book a number of the relevant articles that he has published in various journals and books, and make them available in a more convenient format. These seven older articles and three new ones comprise the present collection, and though written as independent essays, taken together, give a fairly comprehensive view of the Byzantine mind.... All the essays, which constitute chapters of the present book, are clearly and simply written, are neatly illuminated by twenty-one plates (black and white), and are supported by notes, by a Greek-English and English Greek glossary, and by an index.

Dr. Cavarnos' approach is not the usual historical, factual, or even sociological approach that one finds in so many books on Byzantine civilization, but rather an approach that centers on Byzantine religiosity. Byzantine philosophy begins with the assumption of religious faith:

"The philosopher must begin with religious faith, if he is to avoid error and attain truth. Also, one's moral and spiritual state — whether one is courageous or cowardly, continent or incontinent, just or unjust, calm or irritable, humble or proud, disposed to love or to hate, and so on — is viewed as quite relevant to the pursuit of philosophical knowledge" (p. 30).

Byzantine art and architecture are also concerned with Christian spirituality:

"The church building and the icon are regarded not merely as objects that delight us, but rather as vivid reminders of a reality beyond themselves, of things transcendent, supernatural, and as potent aids for our inner purification and transformation" (p. 72).

Byzantine music is also shown to be fundamentally

spiritual . . . . And it is pointed out that the beauty that concerns Byzantine hymnody "is the spiritual, not the physical; the latter is brought into the hymns only by way of comparison, as a means of expressing the beauty that is spiritual" (p. 114).

The quotations cited illustrate the flavor of Dr. Cavarnos' approach. It is the approach of one committed to understanding the Byzantine mind from within, not merely from without. As such, it provides the interested reader with an excellent means by which to penetrate deeply into what is meant to be a Byzantine Orthodox Christian, and a useful guide to understanding the tradition of the Greek Orthodox Church even today

Hagia Sophia. 532-7. South View. Constantinople.

MODERN GREEK THOUGHT

THREE ESSAYS DEALING WITH
PHILOSOPHY, CRITIQUE OF SCIENCE,
AND VIEWS OF MAN'S NATURE AND DESTINY

BY

CONSTANTINE CAVARNOS

INSTITUTE FOR BYZANTINE
AND MODERN GREEK STUDIES
115 Gilbert Road
Belmont, Massachusetts

5

MODERN GREEK THOUGHT*

This magnificent little book was long overdue. It will now be possible for the student of modern Greece to have at his disposal for an understanding of modern Greece a brief but comprehensive survey of what we might well call modern Greek intellectual history. It would be correct to call this book unique, because in a thoroughly historical manner and in a crystal-clear language and style it presents the reader with a documented view of modern Greek thought from the middle of the eighteenth century to the present. Dr. Cavarnos works and writes with the background of a professional philosopher, but this book is not just a survey of philosophy; it deals also with many of modern Greece's most prominent intellectuals (philosophers, theologians, scientists, poets, novelists, and others). It is a bold attempt — a unique and pioneering one — to give the reader a perceptive, meaningful, and reliable overview of the modern Greek mind. The result is eminently successful and extremely useful.

The core of *Modern Greek Thought* consists of three essays, only one of which (and that only in part) has previously been published. The selected bibliography, arranged alphabetically by categories, enables the reader to pursue the subject further in aesthetics, epistemology, ethics, history of philosophy, logic, metaphysics, philosophy of

---

*Review published in *Diakonia*, Vol. V, No. 1, 1970, pp. 64-66.

education, philosophy of history, philosophy of religion, philosophy of science, social and political philosophy. This also gives an idea of the range of topics over which the author pursues his investigations.

The first essay outlines what he discovers as the principal characteristics of modern Greek philosophy: (a) an existential orientation; (2) personalism ("personality is the highest value, to which everything else is in principle subordinate"); (3) idealism or transcendentalism (with "the affirmation of a reality other than the material, physical world"); (4) the ranking of philosophy above science; (5) the ranking of Christian teaching above philosophy; (6) Christian eclecticism; (7) the use of ancient Greek phisophy as a preparatory discipline and the appropriation of many elements from it; (8) independence of mediaeval Western philosophy; (9) independence of the philosophy of the Middle and Far East. Dr. Cavarnos succinctly and brilliantly analyzes each of these characteristics and concludes that "modern Greek philosophy can best be understood as a continuation of Byzantine philosophy in modern times, a continuation which in general has preserved the existential orientation and distinctive Christian outlook of the Byzantines" (p. 37).

The second essay, "Critique of Science," examines science and general education; internal knowledge and scientific knowledge; scientific materialism; ethics and science; and religion and science. Scientism or negativistic Humanism is shown not to be acceptable to many Greek thinkers, and Nicholas Louvaris is cited as arguing that (1) scientific knowledge is not the only possible form of knowledge; (2) science is not in a position to regulate moral and political life; (3) science can neither prove, nor refute the world of values and its truth. This is a very meaty chapter that will arouse considerable discussion and perhaps even controversy.

The concluding essay on the "Views of Man's Nature and Destiny" follows quite naturally from the previous two and really caps them. The importance of man; potential and actual being of man; soul and body; reason; conscience; the heart; the will; the imagination; the immortality of the soul; and the resurrection of the body are examined with respect to the role that they play in writers both religious and secular, and Dr. Cavarnos emerges with a picture of modern Greek thought as essentially Greek Orthodox thought. Perhaps the quotation from Nikephoros Theotokos amply epitomizes this view: "Man is the most remarkable of all God's creatures. He is the creature that more than all others has manifested the infinite wisdom and power of God" (p. 57). The emphasis is on man's creation in the image and likeness of God — "an image of God as regards the powers of the soul, and a likeness of God as regards the achievements of virtue" *(ibid.)*. The final purpose of man's creation is viewed in terms of what the Byzantines called *theosis,* "man's deification, his union with God, his participation in God's perfection and blessedness" (p. 58).

The reader is left with the profound impression that modern Greek thought is essentially Christian in outlook, and specifically Orthodox in orientation. Some observers will dispute this, but they will be hard put to counter Dr. Cavarnos' well documented picture. It is a picture that will make for a better understanding of modern Greece, and will be a valuable source of illumination for students of ancient and Byzantine Greek civilization as well.

PLATO'S THEORY OF FINE ART

BY
CONSTANTINE CAVARNOS

*Τέχνην, ὁ τὴν ἀλήθειαν μὴ εἰδώς,
δόξας δὲ τεθηρευκώς, γελοίαν τινά,
ὡς ἔοικε, καὶ ἄτεχνον παρέξεται.*
Φαῖδρος 262c

"ASTIR" PUBLISHING COMPANY
AL. & E. PAPADEMETRIOU
10 LYCURGUS ST.-ATHENS

6

PLATO'S THEORY OF FINE ART*

The present volume concerns itself with a subject that has long been of interest to the author and to students of Greek philosophy and aesthetics. It is Professor Cavarnos' contention that Plato's theory of fine art has great intrinsic value and interest, but has traditionally been misinterpreted in the matter of what it is that art "imitates." Cavarnos has himself carefully examined the original Platonic Greek texts and various English translations and has attempted to present in a systematic way what Plato actually said about fine art in general and about the arts in particular. The three main sections of this little book include an essay entitled "General Theory of Fine Art," originally published in *Philosophy and Phenomenological Research* (June 1953), under the title "Plato's Teaching on Fine Art" (pp. 11-30); "Critique of the Fine Arts" (pp. 31-63), published in the 1971 annual *Philosophia* of the Research Center for Greek Philosophy of the Academy of Athens; and a section of "Selected Passages from Plato's Works on Fine Art and the Beautiful" (pp. 64-80) translated by the author. The notes (pp. 81-92) are primarily text references, and though there is an index, there is no bibliography on a subject that has a very substantial one.

The argument presented here is that "Plato does not condemn true art but only pseudo art; that for him true art

---

*Review published in *Newsletter* of the Classical Association of the Empire State, Vol. X, No. 3, Spring 1974, p. 3.

has as its immediate aim the expression not of the world of phenomena, but of the world of true being, of eternal forms, of supersensible beauty; and that true art, far from being for him immoral, is in the highest degree moral" (p. 30). This is not only a reasonable conclusion, but thoroughly consistent with Plato's overall philosophy. Dr. Cavarnos' survey of Plato's views on architecture, sculpture, painting, the dance, music, literature, rhetoric, stories, comedy, tragedy, lyric and epic poetry clearly indicates that Plato was not condemning the fine arts as such, but forms of art which are not based on wisdom and not directed toward the higher nature of man. All the arts must address "themselves to the higher element in man, the rational faculty, seeking to strengthen this and enable it to transform man's inner and outer discord into harmony, beauty" (p. 62).

There is tremendous interest in art and even in the theory of art in our own time. Needless to say, sooner or later such discussions return to Plato's painstaking examination of the relation of art to truth and morality; and though modern viewers and critics may not agree with Plato's critique, they must inevitably come to grips with it, because it raises very fundamental questions that are still of primary concern to modern man. Dr. Cavarnos' book on *Plato's Theory of Fine Art* can thus be a very valuable resource for the teacher and student who would see the relevance and relation of ancient to modern concerns.

7

PLATO'S VIEW OF MAN

The two main sections of this book were originally written as Francis Bowen Prize Essays at Harvard in 1945 and 1941 respectively, and have been revised and abridged for the current volume, which includes select passages from Plato's Dialogues on Man and on the Human Soul, and notes. It is a creative and original work that contains reference to and comparison with modern philosophers and Christianity in particular, but focuses on philosophic analysis.

Dr. Cavarnos, a student of the late Professors Raphael Demos and John Wild of Harvard, begins his study with the question of philosophic wonder, a wonder that he shows is ultimately rooted in wonder about man and constitutes the real beginning point for philosophers. This philosophic wonder is a wonder that arose out of dissatisfaction, as far as Plato was concerned, "not merely because he was dissatisfied with the material lot of man, or with the knowledge of his time, but because he was dissatisfied with the whole of man's earthly existence, considered from the cognitive, the aesthetic, the ethical, and the religious standpoint" (p. 11). As Professor Cavarnos sees Plato, the philosopher's main concern "is to acquire knowledge – in the stricter sense of the term – about the nature of man, and from this to deduce the final object

---

*Review published in *The Hellenic Chronicle,* July 3, 1975.

PLATO'S VIEW OF MAN

Two Bowen Prize Essays dealing with the Problem of the Destiny of Man and the Individual Life, together with Selected Passages from Plato's Dialogues on Man and the Human Soul.

BY

CONSTANTINE CAVARNOS

INSTITUTE FOR BYZANTINE
AND MODERN GREEK STUDIES
115 Gilbert Road
Belmont, Massachussetts
U.S.A.

of all of man's toils: his supreme good and the necessary means for attaining it" (pp. 15-16). But it is not possible "fully to discern the nature of the soul, unless one has studied and learned what is true and what is false of the whole of existence" (p. 16). So it becomes the philosopher's task to treat of the whole of reality and to possess knowledge and understanding of the whole universe.

Thus, in the first essay, "The Problem of the Destiny of Man" (pp. 9-24), questions of philosophic wonder, immortality, self-knowledge, cosmology, theology and ethics are discussed, and the point is clearly made that since God is Mind, Intelligence, Reason, man ought to live in consonance with reason, because man's goal is "to become as much as possible like God — ought to strive to become himself perfectly orderly" (p. 20) and help his fellow men to do likewise.

In "The Individual Life" (pp. 25-55), Dr. Cavarnos takes up what is certainly a central aspect of Platonic "psychology" and philosophy, namely, the immortality of the soul, and reviews ten Platonic arguments for the soul's immortality and the structure of the soul with its three powers (the rational, the spirited, and the appetitive), and the four main virtues (wisdom, courage, temperance, and justice). In addition, the inversion of the individual life is discussed in terms of the aristocratic, timocratic, oligarchic, democratic, and tyrannic individual (corresponding to five types of government distinguished by Plato). Knowledge, freedom, and responsibility are placed in their Platonic context; and general inversion of life stresses the necessity for self-transformation and individual regeneration.

The discussion is supported by "Selected Passages from Plato's Dialogues on Man and the Human Soul" (pp. 56-77), translated by Dr. Cavarnos himself.

In conclusion, *Plato's View of Man* is a contribution to Platonic studies. It has the merit of thoughtfully, carefully, and provocatively bringing to the reader's attention the very essence of Platonic thought.

8

THE CLASSICAL THEORY OF RELATIONS*

What we have here is a book that grew out of a seminar paper that was originally written for the Harvard Department of Philosophy in 1947 and then developed into a doctoral dissertation by 1948. There is no doubt that Dr. Cavarnos' thesis should have been published a long time ago, though some critics will find it unfortunate that he did not see fit to update the bibliography in the present version and perhaps rewrite the entire main body of the material in a form that would make it more readily accessible to the general reader. In its present form it is a technical treatise that presents Dr. Cavarnos' views of Plato, Aristotle, and Thomism on relations, demonstrating that they have much in common, and rejecting charges presented by certain recent (up to 1946) critics that Plato, Aristotle, and Aristotelianism had ignored the subject of relations or even had denied their existence. In his book, the author also includes discussions of American and English philosophers such as Santayana, Whitehead, Bradley, Russell, McTaggart and Cornford, and strives to clarify the general notion of relation, to discover the major classes of relations and their subdivisions, and how we cognize them. All realms of being are examined from the standpoint of relation.

---

*Review published in the *Newsletter* of the Classical Association of the Empire State, Vol. XIII, No. 2, Winter 1977, p. 3.

THE CLASSICAL THEORY OF RELATIONS

A STUDY IN THE METAPHYSICS OF
PLATO, ARISTOTLE AND THOMISM

BY

CONSTANTINE CAVARNOS

INSTITUTE FOR BYZANTINE
AND MODERN GREEK STUDIES
115 Gilbert Road
Belmont, Massachusetts 02178
U.S.A.

The Classical Theory of Relations

In *The Classical Theory of Relations,* Dr. Cavarnos demonstrates that Plato, Aristotle, and Thomism dealt with relations and (1) the general notion of relation; (2) the analysis of the relational situation; (3) the classification of relations; (4) the ontological status of relations; and (5) the cognition of relations. He posits that Plato, Aristotle, and Thomism agree on most points and that there is what could be described as "fundamentally a continuity of doctrine and a development in relational theory" (p. 103). The classical philosophers, he finds, had a term for relation and a suggestive definition (". . . relation is an entity which holds *from* one thing *to* another"); that the classical theory of relations distinguishes in the relational situation among the *referent,* the *relation,* the *ground,* and the *converse* of the relation; that even though Plato did not attempt a *classification* of relations, Aristotle contributed significantly in this direction, and Aquinas built on this; that relations are self-consistent, irreducible modes of being, and real "in the sense that *not all* of them are *entia rationis,* entities having being only as objects of the mind," that there are many kinds of relations which are extra-mental (especially in Plato).

The Classical Theory of Relations is a book that classicists, philosophers, and theologians will wish to scrutinize, not only for a better understanding of the classical theory of relations, but also for a proper understanding of related topics in metaphysics and epistemology.

A DIALOGUE ON G. E. MOORE'S ETHICAL PHILOSOPHY

TOGETHER WITH AN ACCOUNT OF THREE TALKS WITH
G. E. MOORE ON DIVERSE PHILOSOPHICAL QUESTIONS

BY

CONSTANTINE CAVARNOS

INSTITUTE FOR BYZANTINE
AND MODERN GREEK STUDIES
115 Gilbert Road
Belmont, Massachusetts 02178
U.S.A.

9

A DIALOGUE ON G.E. MOORE'S ETHICAL PHILOSOPHY*

It will seem strange to some readers to find a work on an important British philosopher, George Edward Moore (1873-1958), published by the Institute for Byzantine and Modern Greek Studies, but then the author and the guiding light of the Institute studied this philosopher and met with him early in his career, when he was working on his Harvard doctoral dissertation on *The Classical Theory of Relations*. The first part of the present work, the *Dialogue*, consists of a discussion of Moore's ethical philosophy as contained in his greatest work, *Principia Ethica*. It "seeks to point out and clarify some basic ideas contained in the *Principia* by posing and answering certain questions, commenting on Moore's views, and comparing them with those of two other eminent English philosophers, contemporaries of his, C.D. Broad and W.D. Ross, who participate in the dialogue." The second part of the work, *Three Talks with G.E. Moore*, is more personal and took place in the winter of 1947-1948 at Moore's home in Cambridge, England, when Dr. Cavarnos was a Sheldon Traveling Fellow in Philosophy from Harvard. The latter work reveals certain aspects of the thought and character of G.E. Moore and also Dr. Cavarnos' own interests and orientation in philosophy.

---

*Review published in *The Hellenic Journal*, October 2, 1980, under the title: "Greek Scholar Sheds Light on British Philosopher."

The dialogue form, undoubtedly influenced by Dr. Cavarnos' early familiarity with Plato (*A Dialogue between Bergson, Aristotle, and Philologos* first reflects this) is used here to focus on G.E. Moore and contrast his views with those of Broad and Ross.

The observations and technical arguments of the work would certainly interest the professional philosopher, but mean little to others. We do learn that Moore raised important questions: "What kind of *things* ought to exist for their own sakes?" that is, "are good in themselves," or "have *intrinsic* value?" Also, "What kind of *actions* ought we to perform?" meaning: "What is 'right action' or duty?" From these questions arises a third: "What is the nature of the *evidence* by which alone any ethical proposition can be proved or disproved, confirmed or rendered doubtful?"

Moore sees the science of ethics as one which "investigates assertions about that property of things which is denoted by the term 'good' and the converse property denoted by the term 'bad.'" "Ethics," he insists, "must enquire not only what things are universally related to goodness, but also, what this predicate (goodness or good), to which they are related, is."

We are soon introduced to his use of "non-naturalistic" and "naturalistic," and are informed that "Each *natural* characteristic of a natural object could be conceived as existing *in time all by itself,* and every natural object is a whole whose parts are its natural characteristics, whereas a 'non-natural' characteristic of a natural object is one which *cannot* be conceived as existing in time all by itself, but only as the property of some natural object." Moore is clear in arguing that the "non-natural" characteristic cannot be discovered by inspecting sense data or introspecting experience, and "it is not definable in terms of characteristics of which one could be aware in those ways together with the notions of cause and substance." He saw that "there is *a vast variety of* great *intrinsic goods* and great *intrinsic evils,*" which almost all involve consciousness of an object and an emotional attitude toward this object. His "principle of organic unities" says that "a whole may possess value in a degree different from that which is obtained by merely summing the degrees in which its parts possess it."

In the *Talks,* Moore holds that all the traditional arguments for the existence of God are unsound. He has none of his own to offer, and knows no possible way of proving the immortality of the mind except the experimental, scientific one. Also, he left unanswered the question of the mind-body or soul-body relationship. And he was surprised to learn of Dr. Cavarnos' work on the subject of relation in Plato *(pros allo)* and Aristotle *(pros ti),* remarking that Plato and Aristotle did not have terms for the notion of relation. It is pointed out that Moore changed his mind on a number of subjects in philosophy on which he had written.

This book shows what many critics of Constantine Cavarnos have already observed, namely, his ability to present even the most complex thinker's work clearly, concisely, and precisely to a general audience.

ΚΩΝΣΤΑΝΤΙΝΟΥ Π. ΚΑΒΑΡΝΟΥ

ΦΙΛΟΣΟΦΙΚΑ ΜΕΛΕΤΗΜΑΤΑ

Μὲ θέματα Ἠθικῆς, Μεταφυσικῆς καὶ Αἰσθητικῆς

INSTITUTE FOR BYZANTINE
AND MODERN GREEK STUDIES
115 Gilbert Road
Belmont, Massachusetts 02178
U.S.A.

10

PHILOSOPHICAL STUDIES*

Philosophical Studies (Philosophika Meletemata), a collection of five essays previously published over a period of ten years (1966-1976), gives an excellent idea of Constantine Cavarnos' interests and concerns as a professionally trained philosopher and a committed Orthodox Christian. The five essays reproduced here are not randomly selected, but form an integrated whole held together by their central theme of the inner man, the soul, its powers and cultivation, liberation from the passions and vices and the acquisition of the virtues, of spiritual beauty. This small book is directed at all those who have philosophic concerns, especially those who are concerned with the question of the nature and destiny of man and desire to live a fuller, higher, more harmonious life. For those interested in the little known area of modern Greek philosophy, there is the opportunity to learn about three important modern Greek thinkers: Benjamin of Lesvos, John N. Theodorakopoulos, and Photios Kontoglou discussed in three of the essays, and two others: Peter Vrailas-Armenis and Panagiotis A. Michelis, referred to in the others.

The first essay (pp. 11-26) in the collection is entitled "Free Will, Character, and Responsibility," and was originally published in the Greek philosophical journal *Diotima*

---

*Review published in *St. Vladimir's Theological Quarterly*, Vol. 25, No. 2, 1981, pp. 139-141.

4 (1976). It is concerned with the question of determinism "soft" and "hard", and free will. After surveying Plato, Aristotle and modern philosophers, it turns its attention to the Byzantine Church Fathers, whose position on the matter is clearly described (man has freedom of the will to make the choice for love of the good and beautiful, and rejection of the evil and base). In the Byzantine view, the individual is responsible for exercising "katharsis" – cleansing of oneself from inclinations toward sin, purification of the passions, and cultivation of one's moral powers. This prepares the individual for the full development of the virtues – accomplished not alone, but with the help of God – , and for the ultimate human goal, *theosis*. The same essay contrasts atheistic with Christian existentialism, but always the main theme is free will with emphasis on its Christian manifestation.

In the second essay (pp. 27-36), "The Metaphysics of Benjamin of Lesvos," originally published in the periodical *Lesviaka* (1966), we are introduced to a modern Greek educator and philosopher who had, among other works, published *Elements of Metaphysics* (Vienna, 1920), though he is perhaps better known for his work in physics and mathematics. Dr. Cavarnos shows how he distinguished between those sciences concerned with the physical world, and metaphysics, which deals with the soul and its powers. The immaterial, indestructible, rational, independent, and free nature of the soul is discussed. And the influence of Orthodoxy, the ancient Greeks, certain European philosophers (particularly John Locke) on Benjamin are especially noted. Benjamin asserts that man was created in the image of God and that man has the power of free choice. He criticizes rationalism and cites John the Damascene, St. John Chrysostom, and Maximos the Confessor. Also, he argues for the immortality of the soul and the existence of God.

In the third essay (pp. 37-48), "John N. Theodorakopoulos: Concerning the Soul," published in the book *Desmos: Dedication to J. N. Theodorakopoulos* by Parnassos (Athens, 1975), Dr. Cavarnos culls that distinguished contemporary Greek philosopher's works for his views on the soul, especially his "Philosophy and Psychology" [in *Archives of Philosophy and Theory of the Sciences* (1929)]; "Concerning the Soul" in the book *Philosophical Essays and Christianity* (1949, 1973); his university lecture notes on *General Psychology* (1956); and his *System of Philosophical Ethics* (1947). Influenced by Kant early in his career, Theodorakopoulos becomes more and more Platonic and Christian in his orientation. Soul is for Theodorakopoulos "a rational unity," "a spiritual existence," "a personal presence of spirit." It is not simply a rational essence, but a moral and religious one as well, having the basic powers of (1) mental perception; (2) will; (3) sensation; (4) imagination; (5) representation; (6) emotion. Through its powers the soul opens the ways to knowledge, action, creativity, and religion. The soul is dynamic, multi-powered, immortal. Through that power of the soul that we call will, we freely make decisions after the suggestion of the mind, and then we proceed to action.

In the fourth essay (pp. 49-61), "The Aretology of Photios Kontoglou," first published in the book *Memory of Kontoglou* by "Astir" Publishing Co. of Athens in 1975, the distinguished iconographer whom Professor Cavarnos knew well personally and whose works he has studied intensively, is revealed through his writings as much concerned with the virtues of simplicity, humility, faith, piety, hope, courage, and love. In Christ he saw the simplicity which Christ demands of every Christian. Through humility, a virtue more referred to than any other, the individual can become God-like. Faith, the gift of illumination of God, he saw as opening the gate of the Kingdom of God. Piety is a "movement of the heroic soul which is not deceived by the false make-up of the world . . . , but clearly and fearlessly sees that there is no salvation possible apart from the narrow path" of piety (p. 54). Hope derives from faith, and it is hope in God, in His mercy, in salvation that Kontoglou emphasizes. True hope is indispensable for inner peace and the real happiness of human beings. Courage has its source in faith and is strengthened by piety, hope, and Christian love, according to Kontoglou. The heroic life is truly the only life of the true Christian, and love is the greatest of all virtues. Dr. Cavarnos presents us with a side of Kontoglou the iconographer that we need to know more of. Kontoglou also speaks of prudence, justice, temperance, chastity, modesty, meekness, and compassion – all within an Orthodox framework. He urges the practice of virtues, emphasizes the free will of the individual, and exhorts all to struggle, to be free from evil.

The final essay (pp. 62-72), on "Spiritual Beauty," first appeared in a commemorative volume for Pangiotis A. Michelis, *In Memoriam Panayotis A. Michelis,* published by the Greek Society of Aesthetics at Athens in 1972. In a breath-taking but eloquent survey of the notion of beauty in Plato, Plotinos, St. Augustine, Descartes, Jonathan Edwards, Ralph Waldo Emerson, Alfred North Whitehead, Theodore of Edessa, St. Basil, St. Gregory Palamas, the Byzantine hymnographers, Niketas Stethatos, St. Symeon the New Theologian, St. John Climacos, and Panagiotis A. Michelis, Dr. Cavarnos establishes the point that whereas the classical anthropocentric notion of beauty is familiar to so many, it must not be forgotten that the Byzantine theocentric tradition emphasized the "higher" beauty, the inner beauty of the soul, of the inner man who has been created in the image of the supreme beauty, God. *Philosophical Studies* will provide the reader with ample material for noting the relation between philosophy and religion, particularly ancient Greek and Western philosophy with the Byzantine Orthodox Christian tradition. There is much here that is worth reading and pondering on. There is much to suggest that the Byzantine tradition is alive and well in a significant number of modern Greek thinkers.

ΚΩΝΣΤΑΝΤΙΝΟΥ Π. ΚΑΒΑΡΝΟΥ
Καθηγητοῦ Πανεπιστημίου

Η ΠΕΡΙ ΠΑΙΔΕΙΑΣ ΘΕΩΡΙΑ ΤΟΥ ΒΕΝΙΑΜΙΝ ΛΕΣΒΙΟΥ

ΕΚΔΟΣΕΙΣ
"ΟΡΘΟΔΟΞΟΥ ΤΥΠΟΥ,,
ΚΑΝΙΓΓΟΣ 10 - 10677 ΑΘΗΝΑΙ

1984

11

THE EDUCATIONAL THEORY OF BENJAMIN OF LESVOS*

The life, thought, and work of Benjamin of Lesvos had previously been dealt with by Professor Cavarnos in his books *Symbols and Proofs of Immortality (Athanatou Zoes Symbola kai Endeixeis)* and *Philosophical Studies (Philosophika Meletemata)*, which were published at Athens in 1964 and 1979, respectively. The present little book is a result of an invitation to participate in the Panhellenic Symposium on Benjamin of Lesvos sponsored by the Greek Ministry of Culture and Science in May of 1982, to which Dr. Cavarnos contributed a paper with the title "The Educational Theory of Benjamin of Lesvos." There is no single work that Benjamin devoted to this subject. Prof. Cavarnos has drawn heavily from a speech delivered on the 18th of January 1818 in Bucharest on the occasion of the inauguration of the Lyceum there, where Benjamin had been invited by John Karatzas, ruler of Wallachia, to reorganize the historic school of Bucharest into a model European Academy. However, Benjamin's speech at Bucharest is not the only source that Dr. Cavarnos draws from. He finds relevant information in Benjamin's *Elements of Arithmetic, Elements of Euclidean Geometry, Elements of Metaphysics*, an announcement concerning his

---

*Review published in *Patristic and Byzantine Review*, Vol. IV, No. 1, 1985, pp. 68-69.

Elements of Ethics (unpublished), and a sermon. Cavarnos describes his own contribution to our understanding of Benjamin as an interpretative synthesis.

Benjamin of Lesvos considered education quite important, not only in terms of the individual, but also in terms of place. His view is an Orthodox Christian one based on the Church Fathers. For him, the purpose of education is for men to actualize their potentialities for rationality and virtue. Through education, man can establish himself as an image and likeness of God in actuality *(energeia)*, instead of remaining such only potentially *(dynamei)*. "In the image" refers to rationality and the power of free choice *(autexousion)*. "In the likeness" refers to virtue *(arete)*. Dr. Cavarnos points out that the home, the church, and the school are the places where education takes place, but also the library, which Benjamin does not mention. Language, history, mythology, geography, and natural history are listed as subjects useful for enriching memory, while for the development of reason he lists "idealogy" (the study of concepts, their sources and relationships), general grammar, logic, arithmetic, geometry, mechanics, astronomy, general physics, specialized physics, chemistry, and ethics. For him, ethics is of all subjects the most valuable and most certain. In his third grouping, Benjamin includes drawing, painting, music, and poetry. Memory, reason, and imagination are all to be cultivated. Attention, order, and proper habituation are forms of discipline that should be part and parcel of an educational program. Dr. Cavarnos explains Benjamin's position on all these subjects in some detail in the chapter called "The Educational Theory of Benjamin of Lesvos" (pp. 7-27).

A special chapter is devoted to the "Ethics of Benjamin of Lesvos" (pp. 28-35). Here we are shown that Benjamin

The Educational Theory of Benjamin 67

follows no philosophic system, but is guided by his Orthodox Christian faith. Biblical and Patristic citations are frequent. Of the ancients, Aristotle is the writer most often referred to. Among others are Plato, Xenophon, Isocrates, Plutarch, Thucydides, Democritos, Homer, and Sophocles.

Prof. Cavarnos has enriched his publication with pertinent texts from the original works of Benjamin (pp. 37-61), including the whole text of his "Speech Concerning Education" (1818), as well as by an appropriate bibliography.

The Educational Theory of Benjamin of Lesvos will be a book of special interest to historians of Orthodox Christian Education, but it will also be a rich source for studying a key figure in the development of modern Greek thought.

Plato   Aristotle

PART II

WORKS ON ORTHODOX CHRISTIAN ART, LIFE, AND THOUGHT

BYZANTINE SACRED MUSIC

The Traditional Music of the Orthodox Church,
Its Nature, Purpose, and Execution

By

CONSTANTINE CAVARNOS

INSTITUTE FOR
BYZANTINE AND MODERN GREEK STUDIES

113 Gilbert Road

Belmont 78, Massachusetts

1

BYZANTINE SACRED MUSIC*

In this brief but significant work, Dr. Constantine Cavarnos brings to the attention of the general reader, as well as of the scholar, the nature, purpose and execution of Byzantine sacred music. In his Preface, he tells us that "The aim of this brief treatise is to give a simple and clear account of the essential characteristics of Byzantine sacred music, the purposes which this music is intended to serve, the spiritual and other conditions requisite for rendering it properly, and the spiritual and other qualifications of Orthodox ecclesiastical chanters."

In the course of his investigation and exposition, he draws upon the New Testament, the writings of the Eastern Church Fathers, the Canons of the Ecumenical Synods, the works of reputable modern historians and students of Byzantine music, as well as from his own investigations and experiences with the churches and monasteries of Greece.

The main part of this treatise is divided into four parts. The first deals with the essential characteristics of Byzantine sacred music, about which he says that it is simple or free from unnecessary complexity, pure or free from everything sensual, ostentatious, insincere, and possessed of unsurpassed power and spirituality. "As regards its outer form or technical aspect, it is characterized by the fact that it is entirely vocal, not making use of any instru-

---

*Review published in *Athene*, Vol. XVII, No. 1, Spring 1956, pp. 40, 43.

ments, and monophonic, that is, employing melodies in one vocal part only" (p. 9).

The second part of this work (pp. 9-15) deals with the aim or purpose of Byzantine music, which is, "in the first place, a means of worship and veneration, and in the second place, a means of self-perfection, of eliciting and cultivating man's higher thoughts and feelings, and of opposing and eliminating his lower, undesirable ones" (p. 10).

The third portion (pp. 15-22)is concerned with the manner in which Byzantine music is executed: "It must, in the first place, be chanted in a state of *attention* or *inner wakefulness*, with *fear of God, devoutness, contrition, humility*" (p. 15). The wholly vocal character of Byzantine music is particularly stressed. It is emphatically and clearly pointed out that musical instruments were excluded by Byzantine ecclesiastical authorities, as well as polyphony or heterophony. Byzantine music, Dr. Cavarnos is very careful to point out, is monophonic or homophonic.

The fourth section of this succinct but important work has to do with the qualifications required of a Byzantine cantor, of whom a stricter manner of life is required than of an ordinary layman (p. 22).

Byzantine Sacred Music also contains an excerpt from a composition by Petros the Peloponnesian, two pages of select statements of the Eastern Church Fathers on psalmody, notes, and an index of proper names.

This book is clearly and concisely written. It should prove to be a valuable introductory handbook to those who are interested in a general introduction to Byzantine music, as well as a starting point for those interested in further study of Byzantine music. In the latter respect, Dr. Cavarnos' notes form a useful reference to literary sources for Byzantine music.

2

BYZANTINE SACRED ART*

In *Byzantine Sacred Art* Dr. Cavarnos has compiled, translated from the Greek, and edited selected writings of the contemporary Greek iconographer Fotis Kontoglou, as well as having written a Preface, the Introduction and Notes. There are eleven beautiful plates that greatly enhance the beauty of this handsome book, a good number of which are of works of Kontoglou himself.

This book, though small in size, exhibits an enormous Orthodox religious fervor. It minces no words in presenting the Orthodox point of view about Byzantine art. Through selections from Kontoglou's writings, Dr. Cavarnos cogently presents the views of Greece's foremost iconographer on Byzantine art and the Byzantine Art Tradition. Comparisons with Western art are constantly made, and the superiority of Byzantine art is categorically asserted. "The most profound kind of painting is religious painting," says Kontoglou, "and the most profound kind of religious painting is the Byzantine, because it is more spiritual, because it has truer roots – the Gospel" (p. 66).

Many books have been written on Byzantine art from the historical and aesthetic points of view, but *Byzantine Sacred Art* is written from the Byzantine spiritual point of view. It is a serious attempt to explain the spiritual art

---

*Review published in *Athene*, Vol. XIX, No. 4, Winter, 1959, p. 11.

Christ the Pantocrator. Ca. 1100. Mosaic in the dome, Church of Daphní, near Athens.

of the Byzantine East to all who would but lend a sympathetic ear.

Some will undoubtedly find this book disturbing, because it has a definite point of view — a Byzantine Orthodox point of view. But it is precisely because Constantine Cavarnos and Fotis Kontoglou have a point of view that they wish to present their point of view to the reading public and clarify the confusion that exists in many people's minds about Byzantine art. This book is not an art manual, nor is it an art history. It is a book that attempts to penetrate into the deeper essence of Byzantine religious art, where there are richer spiritual rewards for those that are but willing to seek them and understand them.

The Second Edition*

The subtitle of this book is: "Selected writings of the contemporary Greek icon painter Fotis Kontoglous on the sacred arts according to the Tradition of Eastern Orthodox Christianity, compiled, translated from the Greek, and edited with a preface, introduction, notes, and illustrations by Constantine Cavarnos." The first edition was published in 1957. This handsome new edition has added twelve new illustrations, new indexes, new chapters, and new material to some of the chapters. The following chapters have been added: "Byzantine Art in Bulgaria;" "A Few Remarks on Russian Iconography;" "Iconography of the Crucifixion;" Hymns of the Passion — Holy Week;" and "Hymnographers and Musicians." Major new texts have been added to the following chapters: "Byzantine

---

*Review forthcoming in *St. Vladimir's Theological Quarterly.*

BYZANTINE SACRED ART

Selected writings of the contemporary Greek icon painter Fotis Kontoglous on the Sacred Arts according to the Tradition of Eastern Orthodox Christianity, compiled, translated from the Greek, and edited with a preface, introduction, notes, and illustrations

By

CONSTANTINE CAVARNOS

Second Edition
Revised and considerably enlarged

INSTITUTE FOR BYZANTINE
AND MODERN GREEK STUDIES
115 Gilbert Road
Belmont, Massachusetts 02178
U. S. A.

Art;" "Byzantine Iconography: A General Historical Survey;" "Byzantine Iconography on Mount Athos;" "Byzantine Art in Yugoslavia;" "Iconography;" "Architecture;" and "Music."

Byzantine Sacred Art remains an anthology of Greece's leading icon painter on the nature and scope of the sacred arts of Byzantium. Books, periodicals and newspapers going back as far as 1923 were culled to provide a coherent picture of Fotis Kontoglou's views. Dr. Cavarnos remarks in his Introduction that Kontoglou "speaks as a religious painter and thinker who experiences profoundly the Byzantine spirit – the ascetic and mystical spirit of Greek Orthodoxy" (p. 17), and for whom "Byzantine iconography is "the art of arts" *(Ibid.)*. Cavarnos also stresses that "Byzantine iconography has a religious function. It seeks to express spiritual things in order thereby to help man penetrate the mysteries of the Christian religion; it seeks to help man rise to a higher level of being, to lift his soul to the blessedness of God" *(ibid)*.

What Dr. Cavarnos has done is to present the reader with the powerful words of a practicing artist who was also an outstanding modern Greek writer, one deeply moved by the beauty, the simplicity, the clarity, the restraint, and the power of Byzantine art, and who himself continued the tradition of that art in an excellent way through his own work and that of his students throughout Greece and elsewhere. Kontoglou knew Western art and thinking as well, so that he could make comparisons that are based on his own artistic, educational, and theological experience. But Kontoglou, like Cavarnos, has a definite Orthodox point of view, rooted in the Byzantine Orthodox religious tradition.

Kontoglou asserts that "Byzantine iconography has

universal significance. This is why, instead of growing old with the passage of time and losing its significance, on the contrary it becomes increasingly new. Byzantine iconography is eternal, like the Gospels, in which it has its source" (p. 99).

This exuberance, this absolute firmness of belief in the validity and claims of Byzantine sacred art as the fundamental Christian art, this clarity of vision on the part of Kontoglou, permeates the whole book, as presented by Dr. Cavarnos. It gives an absolutely clear and unequivocal view of the theological and religious underpinnings of the sacred arts of Byzantium that must be taken seriously.

Byzantine Sacred Art is not an art handbook that tries to explain this particular art from an aesthetic point of view; it is a profoundly religious book that attempts and succeeds in putting forth the Byzantine spiritual point of view as it applies to art. It is an essential book for those who would seek to understand the Byzantine mind and the Orthodox Christian tradition. It is no wonder, then, that the first edition of this very favorably reviewed volume was exhausted. We are thankful that an even richer one has replaced it.

3

ORTHODOXY IN AMERICA*

Orthodoxy in America *(He Orthodoxia sten Amerike)* is essentially a lecture that was delivered at the Institute of Balkan Studies on the 16th of December 1957, when its author was a Fulbright Research Professor in Greece. Portions of the lecture were published in various Greek newspapers of Thessaloniki of December 18, 1957 *(Makedonia, Hellenikos Borras, Phos)*, and *in toto* in the Athens newpaper *Bradyne* (January 16, 17, 18, 1958).

Dr. Cavarnos was addressing a Greek audience that was much interested in the Greek-American situation, so that, even though some mention is made of the Russian, Syrian, and other Orthodox, the emphasis, indeed the experience of the author was and is primarily with the Greek Orthodox Church in America. Immediately preceding the publication of this booklet, he had for several years been a professor at the Holy Cross Greek Orthodox School of Theology, to which he has returned these last few years.

It is particularly interesting to reread this booklet, in view of the enormous changes that have taken place since its publication. In his survey, Dr. Cavarnos had examined the architecture, iconography, music, publications, the situation with the Greek language, the Orthodox theological schools, and the future of the Church in the United States. Since the publication of *Orthodoxy in America,*

---

*Review published in *The Hellenic Chronicle,* November 6, 1980, under the title, "Review in Retrospect."

ΚΩΝΣΤΑΝΤΙΝΟΥ ΚΑΒΑΡΝΟΥ
Διδάκτορος τῆς Φιλοσοφίας τοῦ Πανεπιστημίου Χάρβαρντ
τ. Καθηγητοῦ τῆς Φιλοσοφίας στὸ Πανεπιστήμιο τῆς Βορείου Καρολίνας

Η ΟΡΘΟΔΟΞΙΑ

ΣΤΗΝ ΑΜΕΡΙΚΗ

ΑΘΗΝΑ
1958

a great deal of consciousness raising has developed and been cultivated as to what constitutes legitimate Byzantine Orthodox art, music, theology, and education. Orthodox publications in English and other languages now abound. Though the Greek language may be spoken and understood by fewer and fewer Greek Orthodox Americans, more and more genuine interest in the Church and its life is in evidence. There has been a significant change in the hierarchy of the Church, and fundamental changes in its administrative structure. Personnel have changed, attitudes have changed, and the theologians, philologists, historians, and other intellectuals of Greece and of the Greek government have come to realize that they can be supportive of the Greek Orthodox Church in America, but they cannot determine its direction.

One thing will perhaps please Dr. Cavarnos: there is more known now by Americans of the Greek Orthodox faith about that faith than was known when *Orthodoxy in America* was printed. Perhaps in its own way that publication, by its rigorous criticism of the situation in the 1950's, helped bring about the improved situation of the 1970's and 1980's.

ANCHORED IN GOD

AN INSIDE ACCOUNT OF
LIFE, ART, AND THOUGHT
ON THE HOLY MOUNTAIN OF ATHOS

BY
CONSTANTINE CAVARNOS

"ASTIR,, PUBLISHING COMPANY
AL. & E. PAPADEMETRIOU
10 LYCURGUS ST. — ATHENS

4

ANCHORED IN GOD*

Anchored in God was one of two books which resulted from two academic years which Dr. Cavarnos spent in Greece as Fulbright Research Professor at the University of Athens. The other, in Greek, *Man and the Universe in American Philosophy*, was an attempt to give Greek readers some notion of the greatest American thinkers in philosophy. *Anchored in God* is actually the result of three trips to the Holy Mount of Athos undertaken by Cavarnos in 1952, 1954, and 1958.

The avowed purpose of these trips was to study Eastern Orthodox monasticism in its most living and purest form, and at the same time improve his knowledge and understanding of the liturgical arts of Orthodoxy by getting to meet these arts first hand through direct contact with Byzantine architecture, iconography, and music.

Some of the questions that Dr. Cavarnos asked himself are as follows: "What precisely are the aims of Athonite monasticism, and what are the means that are employed by the monks for achieving them? What is the relationship of these ends and means to the teaching of Christ, St. Paul, and the Eastern Christian Church Fathers? How are the monasteries and smaller monastic establishments

---
*Review published in *Balkan Studies*, Vol. 3, No. 1, 1962, pp. 223-224.

on the Holy Mountain organized? What is the nature and extent of private prayer and common worship? What, besides these, constitutes the monks' daily round of activities? Is the ancient tradition of Eastern Orthodox mysticism known as hesychasm still alive on Athos? What books do the monks especially study and recommend? What are their views on monasticism, contemporary mankind, philosophy, solitude, hardship, fasting, prayer, etc.? What is the exact nature of the architecture, painting, and music on Athos, and what part do these play in the life of the monk?"

These are a few of the questions that Dr. Cavarnos enumerates in his Preface, questions to which he sought vivid and authoritative answers through personal contact with monastic life and with the Athonite monks themselves.

Anchored in God is profusely illustrated by leading artists of Greece such as Fotis Kontoglou and Rallis Kopsidis, and every effort has been made to present Athonite Monasticism in as vivid and lucid a manner as is humanly possible. The intimate form of the personal diary in which the book is written makes this book eminently readable by all persons, no matter what their previous preparation or background.

The twenty monasteries and other monastic establishments of Mount Athos are described intimately but non-technically in thirty-five fascinating chapters which take the reader on a vicarious trip to the greatest center of Eastern Orthodox monasticism. A useful glossary and an index are included at the end of this book.

Anchored in God fulfills its purpose admirably and could serve as an excellent guide to Mount Athos, since each chapter could easily be read as a separate, independent unit. Renewed interest in Mount Athos will certainly stimulate readers to peruse Dr. Cavarnos' contribution with interest and pleasure.

The Second Edition*

Originally published by "Astir" Publishing Company in Athens in 1959, *Anchored in God* has experienced wide popularity in religious circles and has long been out of print. It now becomes available in its original form with some minor changes. Together with the author's companion volume, *The Holy Mountain* (1973), it constitutes a rich and reliable source on Mount Athos for the serious student of Eastern Orthodox Christian monasticism and the ascetic life. Through both works the reader can begin to understand the nature of Orthodox monasticism, and to appreciate a major active surviving religious institution of Byzantium and the only Christian monastic republic in the world.

Dr. Cavarnos' own words excellently describe Athos' purpose: "The monks live quietly, unhurriedly, peacefully, in the midst of unusually beautiful and healthy natural surroundings and in buildings that have been designed, not for the sake of bodily ease or vain display, but for the perfecting of the soul and the glorification of God. Life here has a simplicity, order, sincerity, meaningfulness and depth that it very seldom has in modern secularized society. Free from the confusion, distractions, anxiety and greed of contemporary civilization, the monks

---

*Published in *St. Vladimir's Theological Quarterly*, Vol. 20, No. 3, 1976, pp. 184-185.

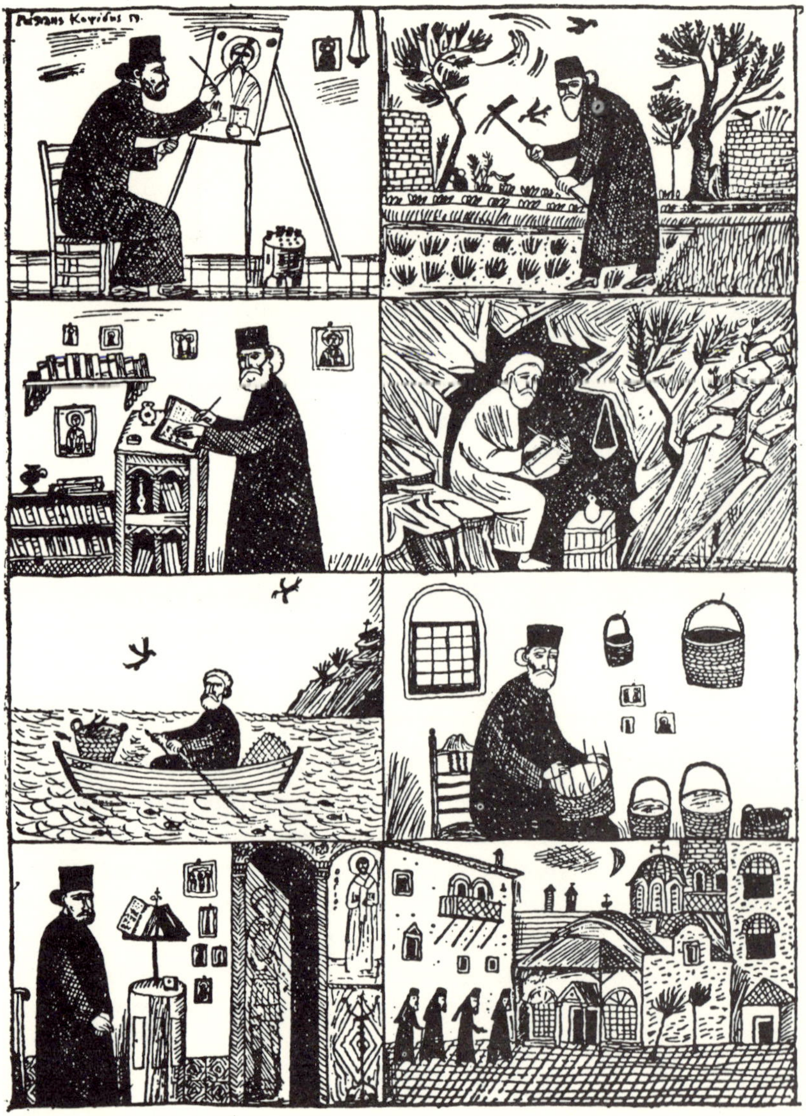

devote themselves to their simple tasks if they live in monasteries, to agriculture or handicrafts if they live in other monastic establishments, and above all to prayer. For those in 'the world', their mode of life is a great lesson in simple, harmonic living, in dedication to spiritual values, in constant striving for self-perfection and union with God" (p. 213.)

Anchored in God is crisply written in thirty-five concise chapters plus a preface, supported by seventy-four illustrations (with contributions from Pericles Papachatzedakis, Fotis Zachariou, Fotis Kontoglou, Rallis Kopsidis, and Nicholas Moutsopoulos), a glossary, and an index . . . . Practical information and observations are generously interlaced with records of monastic conversation and quotations from monastic spiritual literature.

Anchored in God has already proved its worth and with its reissuance now, even though it was originally written seventeen years ago, we continue to have a reliable, vivid, practical, and even personal introduction to the spiritual community of Mount Athos.

THE HOLY MOUNTAIN

Two lectures on Mount Athos, of which the first deals with its Scholars, Missionaries and Saints, and the second with its Music, Musicians, and Hymnographers; together with an account of a Recent Visit to Athos

BY

CONSTANTINE CAVARNOS

Institute for Byzantine
and Modern Greek Studies
115 Gilbert Road
Belmont, Massachusetts 02178
U. S. A.

5

THE HOLY MOUNTAIN*

Anyone familiar with the work of Dr. Constantine Cavarnos knows the prodigious service he has rendered and continues to render to those interested in and committed to Orthodox Christianity and Byzantine and Modern Greek studies. His latest book has all the fine characteristics of previous volumes: clarity of written expression, a straightforward, economical style, well ordered organization, and firm grounding in primary sources. This is his second book on Mount Athos (*Anchored in God*, originally published in Athens in 1959, has experienced excellent circulation and wide acclaim) and is an important contribution to Athonite bibliography. The three major portions of the book have been well rehearsed and well researched. Part One, "Scholars, Missionaries, and Saints," was originally delivered as a lecture at Yale University on October 21, 1968, sponsored by the Yale Orthodox Christian Movement; Part Two, "Music, Musicians, and Hymnographers," was written for the Colgate International Students Forum and the Colgate Orthodox Christian Fellowship Symposium on Mount Athos on May 15, 1969, and considerably augmented for publication. Part Three, "Recent Visit to Athos," was written in 1965, when the author last visited the Holy Mountain and added significant new material that had not been included in his

---

*Published in *Balkan Studies*, Vol. 15, No. 2, 1974, pp. 350-352.

previous work on Mount Athos. In addition, notes a "Menologion of Athonite Saints" (a list of the saints of the Mountain according to the months when their memory is celebrated), a glossary, a bibliography, and an index round out this conveniently arranged volume.

It is perhaps important to point out that this book includes the first comprehensive survey of the scholars, missionaries and saints of Mount Athos and the first attempt to discuss the music, musicians, and hymnographers of Athos in a somewhat extensive and systematic manner. The 1965 pilgrimage conveys communications from the Holy Mount regarding the monastic attitude toward "Ecumenism," Orthodox monasticism in the contemporary world, and other subjects. The Menologion makes available for the first time a convenient listing of Athonite saints.

The beauty of *The Holy Mountain* is the absolutely lucid way in which the material is presented — with a clarity that even the most uninitiated lay reader can understand, but also with a sincerity and authority that any scholar will appreciate and churchman respect. Dr. Cavarnos knows his subject well — not merely in publications, but as a living tradition which he himself has lived, and continues to respect and study. In a secular world and a secular Church that often misunderstand the purpose and mission of this largest community of Orthodox Christian monks anywhere, he seeks to interpret their message as it involves "avoidance of the world, self-concentration, dedication to love of God and the keeping of His commandments through strict bodily and spiritual purity" (Archimandrite Gabriel of Dionysiou Monastery). Dr. Cavarnos cites Abbot Gabriel who emphasizes that it was Basil the Great, the teacher and organizer of Eastern Orthodox-

ST. GREGORY PALAMAS
Fresco, Monastery of Dionysiou.
XVIth century.

monasticism *par excellence,* who exhorted the monks "to withdraw from the world, and to have as their mission an entirely exemplary life, so that through it the monastic life might be praised and the name of God be glorified.... Orthodox Monasticism has for its mission . . . devotion to God, love towards Him in the first place, and in the second place love towards men, which it practices towards monastics, especially within brotherhoods, and towards pilgrims and visitors who come to the holy monastic establishments . . . ." (p. 118).

A book like *The Holy Mountain* needs to be studied in the light of the history of Eastern Christianity and the contemporary world. An anti-monastic spirit pervades our age, and the madness of tourism permeates every aspect of modern Greek life and now even threatens to make inroads on Mount Athos. The number of men committing themselves to a religious life on the Holy Mountain is growing smaller. Nevertheless, there are many Greeks, Russians, Serbians, Bulgarians, and Rumanians who have infused Mount Athos with their own spiritual lives. They have ensured, in the words of Father Theocletos of Dionysiou, that "the Holy Mountain will always remain as it is, a place of repentance, of purification and of incessant praising of the Lord, and a Monastic Center that continues the ancient monastic tradition of the Orthodox Church" (p. 131).

This work on Mount Athos will not only provide the interested reader with valuable information, but may even open up religious vistas and understanding of the nature of Orthodox Christian monastic life never before realized, experienced, or understood. No student of Orthodox Christianity and no Orthodox Christian should pass this book by.

ΚΩΝΣΤΑΝΤΙΝΟΥ ΚΑΒΑΡΝΟΥ

ΑΦΙΕΡΩΜΑ ΣΤΟ ΜΟΝΑΣΤΗΡΙ ΤΗΣ ΕΥΑΓΓΕΛΙΣΤΡΙΑΣ ΤΟΥ ΠΛΩΜΑΡΙΟΥ ΤΗΣ ΛΕΣΒΟΥ

Τὸ ἱστορικὸ τοῦ Μοναστηριοῦ, μαζὶ μὲ ἕνα Λόγο γιὰ τὸν Ὀρθόδοξο Μοναχισμὸ καὶ σοφὲς παρατηρήσεις Νεοελλήνων Ἁγίων καὶ Λογίων γιὰ τὴν Μοναχικὴ Ζωή.

ΑΘΗΝΑΙ 1970

6

THE CONVENT OF EVANGELISTRIA*

Offering to the Convent of Evangelistria of Plomarion, Lesvos *(Aphieroma sto Monasteri tes Euangelistrias tou Plomariou Lesbou)*, with a laudatory Prologue by the Metropolitan of Mytilene Iakovos, is a brief description of a monastery founded in 1919 by the hieromonk Chrysanthos Papageorgantis of Trigonas, Lesvos, that functioned as a convent with ten or twelve nuns for a decade. It is now in a state of disrepair, and since 1965 Dr. Cavarnos and others on the island of Lesvos have made a serious effort to restore this monastic complex to its original purpose. The other two sections of this booklet consist of a discourse by the author outlining the nature of Orthodox monasticism, with ample documentation from Biblical sources (both Old and New Testaments), and a collection of passages from modern Greek saints and scholars on monasticism, from St. Cosmas Aitolos (1714-1779) to the contemporary monk Theocletos of Dionysiou, author of *Between Heaven and Earth*.

This book is clear evidence of Dr. Cavarnos' continuing missionary and scholarly zeal in making Greek Orthodox spirituality well known to the contemporary secular world on both sides of the Atlantic.

---

*Review published in *St. Vladimir's Theological Quarterly*, Vol. 16, No. 1, 1972, pp. 45-46.

7

SYMBOLS AND PROOFS OF IMMORTALITY*

The profusely illustrated book, *Symbols and Proofs of Immortality (Athanatou Zoes Symbola kai Endeixeis)*, is a kind of offering by Dr. Cavarnos to the place of his ancestral origin, Plomarion, in the southern part of the famous island of Lesvos. There, beginning in August of 1961, he set upon a pilgrimage to visit, worship at and investigate the churches of the island, even though they were post Byzantine. It was his purpose to determine to what extent the builders, architects, and the iconographers of the island followed the Byzantine tradition of the Greek Orthodox Church. In 1962, the president of the Plomaritan Society of Professional Men "Benjamin of Lesvos," Dr. Basil Topalis (M.D.), exhorted him to organize the results of his investigations and lecture on them to that society. Subsequently, Dr. Topalis and other esteemed friends encouraged him to publish his observations. In the course of his research, he discovered the works *Concerning the Existence and Immortality of the Soul* by the Plomaritan Metropolitan Gregory of Lesvos, *The Elements of Metaphysics* by Benjamin of Lesvos, and the *Codex of the Orthodox Christian Faith* by the Metropolitan of Plomari Constantine Koidakis. It seemed good to him to add a second part to his book, where there would be edited selections from these sources in which the existence and

---

*Review published in *The Greek Orthodox Theological Review*, Vol. XI, No. 2, Winter 1965-1966, pp. 281-282.

ΚΩΝΣΤΑΝΤΙΝΟΥ Π. ΚΑΒΑΡΝΟΥ
τ. ΚΑΘΗΓΗΤΟΥ ΤΗΣ ΦΙΛΟΣΟΦΙΑΣ ΣΤΟ ΠΑΝΕΠΙΣΤΗΜΙΟ ΤΗΣ ΒΟΡΕΙΟΥ ΚΑΡΟΛΙΝΑΣ

ΑΘΑΝΑΤΟΥ ΖΩΗΣ
ΣΥΜΒΟΛΑ ΚΑΙ ΕΝΔΕΙΞΕΙΣ

Προσκύνημα στοὺς Ναοὺς τῆς Ἐπαρχίας Πλωμαρίου Λέσβου. Θεώρησις τῆς Ἀρχιτεκτονικῆς καὶ τῶν Εἰκόνων τους. Ἡ περὶ Ψυχῆς καὶ Ἀθανασίας διδασκαλία Βενιαμὶν τοῦ Λεσβίου, Μεγάλου Διδασκάλου τοῦ Γένους, Γρηγορίου τοῦ Λεσβίου, Μητροπολίτου Δρυϊνουπόλεως, καὶ τοῦ Κωνσταντίνου Κοϊδάκη, Μητροπολίτου Πλωμαρίου.

ΕΚΔΟΤΙΚΟΣ ΟΙΚΟΣ «ΑΣΤΗΡ»
ΑΛ. & Ε. ΠΑΠΑΔΗΜΗΤΡΙΟΥ
ΟΔΟΣ ΛΥΚΟΥΡΓΟΥ 10 — ΑΘΗΝΑΙ — 1964

ΝΑΟΙ ΕΠΑΡΧΙΑΣ ΠΛΩΜΑΡΙΟΥ

Ὁ Ἅγιος Ἰγνάτιος, ἐπίσκοπος Μηθύμνης.
Φορητὴ εἰκόνα στὸν ναὸ τῆς Μεταμορφώσεως.

immortality of the soul and the after-life are discussed in philosophical or theological terms. These selections were consequently added with introductions and comments, in the belief that not only were these writers closely connected with Plomarion, but their works were also expressive of some of the fundamental doctrines of Orthodoxy which the icons and the churches of the island embody. The book thus contains two parts that may be used separately or read together. Both are lucidly written and carefully edited guides for the general reader.

The first part of the book (pp. 15-118), "Symbols and Indications of Immortal Life," provides the reader with precise, concise, up-to-date chapters (15 in all) in non-technical language of the churches in Trigonas, Melies, Plagia, St. Isidoros, Plomarion, Mesouna, Kato Chorio, Megalochori, Kournela, Palaiochori, Drota, Stavros, Ambelico, Akrasi, Neochori, and a number of other smaller locations. Prof. Cavarnos notes with some disappointment the general lack of use of the pure Byzantine Orthodox tradition in the iconography and architecture of the churches, but sees certain encouraging signs of a return to it (e.g., in the Chapel of the Holy Apostles at Trigonas built in 1961). He hopes that responsible natives will see to the proper cleaning and restoration of various genuinely Orthodox manifestations of religious art. The second part of the book (pp. 121-191) will be valuable for those who would like a representative view of Plomaritan theological and philosophical scholarship.

Constantine Cavarnos has now given us another fine book in the general format of his excellent *Anchored in God*.

8

THE QUESTION OF THE UNION OF THE TWO CHURCHES*

The Question of the Union of the Two Churches (To Zetema tes Henoseos ton Dyo Ekklesion) is the substance of a lecture delivered by Dr. Cavarnos on the 22nd of March 1964 (Sunday of Orthodoxy) to the society "Benjamin of Lesvos" at Plomari. It is concerned with the examination of the question: "Is Union of the Roman Catholic and Greek Orthodox Churches possible and, if possible, is such a union desirable?" As the basis for discussion he uses the works of recent Orthodox writers like Saint Nectarios, Saint Nicodemos the Hagiorite, and Athanasios Parios. Dogmatic differences between the two churches are first noted. These are said to consist of the Roman teachings on the primacy and infallibility of the Pope, the *filioque,* the Purgatorial fire, and the immaculate conception of the Virgin Mary. Sacramental differences are noted in the cases of Baptism (asperion as against immersion), in the Eucharist (the use of unleavened as against leavened bread, communion in one species as against both species), in the use of Unction only in extreme situations instead of as a healing Sacrament.

In discussing worship, Dr. Cavarnos notes the fleshly nature of Western iconography, the use of statues, and, in general, the secular spirit of Western Catholicism, and cites the Crusades and the Spanish Inquisition as wholly

---

*Review published in *The Greek Orthodox Theological Review,* Vol. XI, No. 2, Winter 1965-1966, pp. 282-283.

ΚΩΝΣΤΑΝΤΙΝΟΥ ΚΑΒΑΡΝΟΥ
ΚΑΘΗΓΗΤΟΥ ΠΑΝΕΠΙΣΤΗΜΙΟΥ

ΤΟ ΖΗΤΗΜΑ ΤΗΣ ΕΝΩΣΕΩΣ ΤΩΝ ΔΥΟ ΕΚΚΛΗΣΙΩΝ

ΠΡΟΛΟΓΟΣ ΚΑΙ ΕΙΚΟΝΕΣ
Ὑπὸ ΦΩΤΙΟΥ Ν. ΚΟΝΤΟΓΛΟΥ

ΕΚΔΟΣΕΙΣ
«ΠΑΝΕΛΛΗΝΙΟΥ ΟΡΘΟΔΟΞΟΥ ΕΝΩΣΕΩΣ» (Π.Ο.Ε.)
ΑΘΗΝΑΙ 1964

unjustified examples of secular as against spiritual activity. It is Cavarnos' contention that union is neither possible nor desirable, that the differences are basic differences which could not be glossed over by hierarchical administrative fiat, that the Orthodox faithful would not accede to formal negotiations that do not grow out of a real desire of the heart.

The Question of the Union of the Two Churches is an excellent brief summary of the key differences between Greek Orthodoxy and Roman Catholicism. However, it fails to show that there is also a common ground of Christian concern and agreement which deserves exploration in line with the Biblical injunction "that they all may be one" (John 17: 12). Unlike some other really polemical tracts, Dr. Cavarnos does point out quietly that there are serious differences which make present Ecumenical discussions between Catholics and Orthodox more theoretical than real. Surely, all sides should approach these discussions in a spirit of willingness to hear and be heard, without necessarily compromising one's basic beliefs.

ΚΩΝΣΤΑΝΤΙΝΟΥ ΚΑΒΑΡΝΟΥ
ΚΑΘΗΓΗΤΟΥ ΠΑΝΕΠΙΣΤΗΜΙΟΥ

ΕΛΛΑΣ ΚΑΙ ΟΡΘΟΔΟΞΙΑ

ΕΚΔΟΣΕΙΣ
"ΟΡΘΟΔΟΞΟΥ ΤΥΠΟΥ"
ΑΘΗΝΑΙ 1967

9

GREECE AND ORTHODOXY*

It does not take the reader long to discover that Dr. Cavarnos is, theologically speaking, a conservative, nor is this inconsistent with his devotion to the Greek Church Fathers and his insistence that the Byzantine heritage has a real role to play in the life of the modern Orthodox Christian. *Greece and Orthodoxy (Hellas kai Orthodoxia)* is a collection of essays dedicated to the late iconographer, author, and thinker Fotis Kontoglou (1895-1965), a staunch defender of traditional Orthodoxy, a prolific and influential writer, and more than any other single figure in our time responsible for the renascence of Byzantine art as a viable and proper form of religious expression in modern Greece. Professor Cavarnos has known Kontoglou personally, has read and studied his written works, and has spent a great deal of time on his art work as well. As a layman, Kontoglou dedicated his life to the Church of Greece and to the restoration of Byzantine art to an active and creative role in the life of the Orthodox Church. It is no wonder then that six out of the fifteen essays in this collection should be directly concerned with Kontoglou, all of which but one he had read. There can be no doubt that all of the essays in this volume, written in demotic Greek, in one way or another show the influence of an artist who reflected in his own life and work the spirit of Byzantine Orthodoxy.

---

*Review published in *The Hellenic Chronicle,* November 14, 1968.

The essays, written over a period of years extending from 1948 to 1966, are directed to a Greek audience, and many of the essays were originally printed in Greek journals, magazines and newspapers. A few are translated from works originally composed in English by the author and published in the United States. "The Murals of Panselinos" and "El Greco and Byzantine Art" are also found in English translation in more or less the same form in *Byzantine Thought and Art*. The five essays on Kontoglou give a brief conspectus of Kontoglou and his work, and are entitled "Kontoglou and Modern Greek Civilisation;" "Kontoglou and Byzantine Art;" "Kontoglou and Contemporary Times;" "Fotis Kontoglou the Confessor;" and "Life and Works of Fotis Kontoglou." The essays which were obviously of particular interest to Kontoglou are "Orthodoxy and Tradition;" "Byzantine Church Music;" "El Greco and Byzantine Art;" and "The Way to Spiritual Knowledge."

A number of the essays that occur here are perhaps of limited general interest and do not appear in English versions, such as "The Byzantine Museum;" "Byzantine Churches of Greece;" "Theophilos and Byzantine Art;" "The Newly Manifested Saints of Thermi of Lesvos." The short essay on "The Holy Mountain" deserves to appear in English, since it presents a simple but vivid picture of Mount Athos.

Throughout the simplicity, clarity, and power of Byzantine art are emphasized and traditional aspects of Byzantine art, music, theology, and religious practice are presented. The secularism of the modern world and the faithlessness of modern man are pointed out and condemned. Though Kontoglou and Cavarnos may seem strange to some persons, they are spiritual men, children of Byzantine Christianity, who earnestly believe in the preservation of the Byzantine Orthodox tradition, untainted by Western secularism and materialism, and in its creative and recreative powers in the modern world. It is fair to say that the title *Greece and Orthodoxy* gives the volume a kind of unity in that it does give the reader a picture of various aspects of contemporary Greek Orthodoxy.

"There is need of Christian faith, of a Christian ethos, of a Christian life. Faith and a life which is in accordance with faith cleanse the soul and it sees the truth. Internal cleansing is a prerequisite for the apprehension of spiritual truth and for the vision of God" (p. 89). With these words of Dr. Cavarnos one could conclude this review with assurance that the publications of Constantine Cavarnos deserve careful scrutiny, proper study, and sympathetic understanding.

The main church of a monastery, Mount Athos.

ΚΩΝΣΤΑΝΤΙΝΟΥ ΚΑΒΑΡΝΟΥ
Καθηγητοῦ Πανεπιστημίου

Η ΟΡΘΟΔΟΞΟΣ ΠΑΡΑΔΟΣΙΣ ΚΑΙ Ο ΣΥΓΧΡΟΝΙΣΜΟΣ

ΕΚΔΟΣΕΙΣ
«ΟΡΘΟΔΟΞΟΥ ΤΥΠΟΥ»
ΑΘΗΝΑΙ 1971

10

THE ORTHODOX TRADITION AND MODERNIZATION*

Professor Cavarnos has vigorously pursued a policy of gently but firmly defending the Greek Orthodox tradition against increasingly severe attacks and incursions from contemporary secular society. In this small book on *The Orthodox Tradition and Modernization (He Orthodoxos Paradosis kai ho Synchronismos)*, originally delivered as a lecture for the Panhellenic Orthodox Union in Athens on May 27, 1970, he sets out to define and defend the Orthodox tradition against what he believes are certain stultifying modernizing practices and influences. Always he is careful to draw supporting evidence for his defense from Biblical, Patristic and Synodical sources. Those readers already familiar with his numerous writings on Byzantine music and iconography will recognize the arguments and will sympathize with his insistence that the integrity and original beauty and purposes of these ecclesiastical arts be duly preserved and promoted. His comments on preserving traditional physical appearances of the clergy (such as dress, long hair, beard) are much more difficult to defend in truly Christian terms. The matter of de-Hellenization of Christianity is much more serious, and it is too bad that Dr. Cavarnos did not go into greater detail, because it is an issue that deserves to be explored in depth, since it raises the question of the very nature of Chris-

---

*Review published in *The Greek Orthodox Theological Review*, Vol. XVII, No. 2, Fall 1972, pp. 300-301.

tianity. The negative attitude toward Orthodox participation in the Ecumenical Movement is one being increasingly taken by Orthodox churchmen, ironically at a time when the Orthodox churches constitute the largest single bloc in the World Council of Churches, and at a time when Orthodox participation, if prudently directed, could well serve the cause of Orthodox Christianity immensely.

The Orthodox Tradition and Modernization is a well-written reflection of the increasingly conservative direction contemporary Orthodoxy is taking, and representative of a long tradition that insists that traditional Orthodoxy must be preserved in the traditional ways.

At the end of this study, Dr. Cavarnos offers some specific constructive suggestions as to how men both in Greece and America might best adapt the Orthodox tradition to the current scene. These suggestions should be carefully heeded.

11

GREEK LETTERS AND ORTHODOXY*

Originally delivered as a lecture on the occasion of Greek Letters Week at the Taxiarchai Church of Watertown, Massachusetts, on February 7, 1971, *Greek Letters and Orthodoxy (Ta Hellenika Grammata kai he Orthodoxia)* was published in serial form in the weekly *Hellenic Chronicle* from February 18 to May 6, 1971, in English, and in Greek in the Athens *Orthodox Press (Orthodoxos Typos)* from May 15 to September 15, 1971. It is now published as a booklet and made available to a wider audience in a more permanent and convenient form.

Greek Letters and Orthodoxy concerns itself with three topics: the ways in which Orthodoxy was related to Greek Letters from the beginning of the Christian era to the present; whether the relations of Greek Letters to Orthodoxy were good or bad; whether Greek Letters have a value for Orthodoxy today or should be viewed as irrelevant or even injurious to the Orthodox Church.

In clear and precise language, Dr. Cavarnos illustrates the positive role Greek Letters have played, in three chapters entitled: "The Relation of Orthodoxy to Greek Letters;" "The Value of Greek Letters in the Past;" and "The Value of Greek Letters for the Present," respectively. The Greek translation of the Old Testament (the so-called *Septuagint*), the Greek New Testament, the Holy Canons of

---

*Review published in the *Greek World*, Vol. I, No. 6, November-December, 1976, p. 43.

ΚΩΝΣΤΑΝΤΙΝΟΥ Π. ΚΑΒΑΡΝΟΥ
Διδάκτορος τῆς Φιλοσοφίας (Χάρβαρντ)
Καθηγητοῦ Πανεπιστημίου

ΤΑ ΕΛΛΗΝΙΚΑ ΓΡΑΜΜΑΤΑ ΚΑΙ Η ΟΡΘΟΔΟΞΙΑ

Ἡ Σχέσις τοῦ Ὀρθοδόξου Χριστιανισμοῦ πρὸς τὰ Ἑλληνικὰ Γράμματα — Γλῶσσαν, Ἀρχαίαν Φιλοσοφίαν, Ῥητορικὴν καὶ Ποίησιν — καὶ ἡ Ἀξία των δι' αὐτὸν

Μετάφρασις ἐκ τῆς ἀγγλικῆς
ὑπὸ Μιχαὴλ Μαραγγούλα

ΕΚΔΟΣΕΙΣ «ΟΡΘΟΔΟΞΟΥ ΤΥΠΟΥ»
ΑΘΗΝΑΙ 1976

the Seven Ecumenical Synods, the Greek Church Fathers, liturgical books, and writings of theologians of the post-Byzantine period in Greek are referred to as concrete examples of the use of the Greek language. The subject of Greek philosophy is examined for the role it has historically played in the expression of Christian teaching. Cavarnos also surveys the role that the Greek language played in the history of the Orthodox Church and, synoptically, the roles of ancient Greek philosophy, rhetoric and poetry in the history of the Church. Finally, he demonstrates the value of Greek Letters for the contemporary Orthodox Christian by stressing the importance of a knowledge of the Greek language for a proper understanding of Holy Scripture, liturgical books, the Greek Church Fathers, and the contemporary Orthodox of Greece. Ancient Greek philosophy is again shown to be as valuable as ever for a proper comprehension of contemporary Orthodox thought and for a better understanding of philosophy, religion, and other subjects generally. Ancient Greek rhetoric and poetry are also shown to have had special influence on the writings of a number of important post-Byzantine Orthodox writers, as well as on Saint Paul, the Church Fathers, and various theologians.

All in all, Dr. Cavarnos demonstrates, in a reasonable and convincing way, that the Greek language, ancient Greek philosophy, rhetoric, and poetry have played and continue to play an important role for Orthodox Christians, and that every effort should be made to continue the cultivation of Greek Letters.

ORTHODOX
ICONOGRAPHY

Four essays dealing with the History of Orthodox Iconography, the Iconographic Decoration of Churches, the Functions of Icons, and the Theology and Aesthetics of Byzantine Iconography. In addition, three Appendixes containing Authoritative Early Christian Texts on Icons, explanations of the Techniques of Iconography, and a discussion of Two Russian Books on Icons

BY

CONSTANTINE CAVARNOS

INSTITUTE FOR BYZANTINE
AND MODERN GREEK STUDIES
115 Gilbert Road
Belmont, Massachusetts 02178
U.S.A.

12

ORTHODOX ICONOGRAPHY*

Dr. Cavarnos has labored hard and steadily to make traditional Orthodox iconography known through his publications, lectures, and teaching. In this volume he has gathered four essays dealing with the history of Orthodox iconography, the iconographic decoration of churches, the functions of icons, and the theology and aesthetics of Byzantine iconography. In addition, he has included three appendices with authoritative early texts of St. John Damascene and the Seventh Ecumenical Synod on icons, explanations of the techniques of iconography by the renowned Photios Kontoglou, and reviews of two Russian books on icons (Eugene N. Trubetskoi's *Icons: Theology in Color* and Leonide Ouspensky's and Vladimir Lossky's *The Meaning of Icons*). Finally, he has incorporated twenty-five beautiful plates.

The first two chapters on the history of iconography and church decoration were published originally in *The Orthodox Ethos*, edited by A. J. Philippou (Oxford, 1964); the third chapter, on the function of icons, appears here for the first time; the fourth chapter was contained in a long article entitled "Theology and Aesthetics of Byzantine Iconography" in the January-June 1972 issue of the Athenian scholarly journal *Theologia*, whereas the texts of St. John Damascene and the Seventh Ecumenical Synod appeared

---

*Review published in *The Greek Orthodox Theological Review*, Vol. XXIII, No.1, Spring 1978, pp. 87-88.

originally in the pamphlet, *The Icon: Its Spiritual Basis and Purpose* (1955). The translations from Kontoglou are printed here in English for the first time. The review of Trubetskoi's book appeared in *The Greek Orthodox Theological Review* in 1974, while that of Ouspensky's and Lossky's work was published in *Speculum* in 1957.

Addressed to those interested in the Eastern Orthodox Church, *Orthodox Iconography* will be particularly informative to those concerned with the art of painting in its educational and religious uses. Drawing upon not only his personal observations, but also his first-hand knowledge of the writings of the Church Fathers and modern authorities on Orthodox iconography, Dr. Cavarnos emphasizes that "True iconography is intended to take us beyond anatomy and the three-dimensional world of matter to a realm that is immaterial, spaceless, timeless – the realm of the spirit, of eternity. And hence the forms and colors are not those that one customarily observes around him, but have something unworldly about them. The iconographer does not endeavor to give the illusion of material reality, a photographic likeness of men, mountains, trees, animals, buildings, and so on. He gives a schematic representation of these, leaving out everything that is not essential" (pp. 38-39). Clearly, the "icon is *essentially a symbol,* a symbol which is designed to lead from the physical and psychophysical realms to the spiritual realm" (p. 39).

Orthodox Iconography gives the reader the practical and theoretical information that is needed to understand the history, the nature, the function, the purpose, and the value of the icon in Eastern Orthodoxy. Because the icon is directly related to Orthodox religion, its basic efficacy can be tested by how much "we become like that which

St. John the Theologian and his disciple St. Prochoros. 1345. Miniature in a manuscript Book of the Gospels, Monastery of St. John the Theologian, Patmos.

we habitually contemplate." Spiritual ascent, *theosis* (union with God through grace, 'divinization'), and salvation *(soteria)* are involved, because that which promotes spirituality promotes faith, meekness, humility, passionlessness or dispassion *(apatheia)*, and spiritual love. "Love of God is love of Him as the supreme, all-beautiful, all-good, all-perfect personal Being and the aspiration for union with Him by Grace. This union is called *theosis,* 'deification,' and is the final end for which man was created" (p. 45). This is the theology involved in the icon. It must be clearly understood, if a proper appreciation is to be acquired of the icon as a promoter of — and instrument for — the acquisition of the virtues that make man a likeness of God and lead to *theosis.*

Orthodox Iconography is an indispensable resource for every student of Orthodox Christianity and for every Orthodox Christian. Dr. Cavarnos is to be congratulated for presenting us with such a lucid and valuable volume.

13

WAYS AND MEANS TO SANCTITY*

This book was originally presented as a lecture entitled "The Ways of Sanctity" on October 3, 1978, at the Orthodox Theological Seminary of Saint Tikhon of Zadonsk in South Canaan, Pennsylvania, as part of the series "Called to be Saints." It was published in English in May, 1979, in the Seminary's yearbook, *Tikhonaire* (pp. 23-29). A Greek version was published in book form by the spiritual daughters of the late nun Euphrosyne, who was associated with the *Orthodox Press,* a religious weekly published in Athens, and is a fitting memorial to this dedicated woman ascetic. The Greek translation appeared earlier in serial form in the *Orthodox Press* from the 31st of August to the 5th of October in 1979. It has been enlarged by the addition of a prologue, epilogue, amplifications in the main text, indexes, and many hagiographical illustrations.

Ways and Means to Sanctity is a compact, extremely well documented and well written handbook on sainthood: how to recognize it, and how to achieve it! In addition to the introduction and epilogue, the two main parts of this fine book are devoted to "Ways to Sanctity" and "Means to Sanctity."

Dr. Cavarnos traces the idea of the saint back to the Old and New Testaments, with special emphasis to Leviticus 11.44: "Ye shall be sanctified and ye shall be holy, because

---

*Review published in *The Greek Orthodox Theological Review,* Vol. XXVI, No.3, Fall 1981, pp. 237-238.

ΚΩΝΣΤΑΝΤΙΝΟΥ ΚΑΒΑΡΝΟΥ
Καθηγητοῦ Πανεπιστημίου

ΟΔΟΙ ΚΑΙ ΤΡΟΠΟΙ
ΠΡΟΣ
ΤΗΝ ΑΓΙΟΤΗΤΑ

«Ἁγιασθήσεσθε καὶ ἅγιοι ἔσεσθε, ὅτι ἅγιός εἰμι ἐγὼ Κύριος ὁ Θεὸς ὑμῶν».

ΕΚΔΟΣΕΙΣ
"ΟΡΘΟΔΟΞΟΥ ΤΥΠΟΥ„

ΑΘΗΝΑΙ, 1980

Ways and Means to Sanctity

I, the Lord your God, am holy;" (also, Leviticus 19.2 and 20.7) and Matthew 5.48: "Be ye perfect, even as your Father who is in heaven is perfect" ("perfect" = "holy"). In the Orthodox tradition, "a saint is a person who has become a partaker of Divine grace and is inspired and guided by the Holy Spirit. Such a person is free from every vice and a possessor of all the virtues" (p. 10). In Dr. Cavarnos' words, "The partaking of the grace of the Holy Spirit, union with the divine energies, sanctification, is called *theosis*, 'deification' or 'divinization.' He who attains *theosis* becomes united with God, and thereby participates in God's perfection and blessedness" (p. 11). This is the goal of all humanity, not simply of the Orthodox saint. The saint is described in Patristic writings as possessing faith, patience, humility, and spiritual love. Dr. Cavarnos analyzes each one of these virtues with particular reference to the Church Fathers.

Throughout his study, he utilizes Patristic sources, including the five (Saint Peter Damascene) or six (Saint Nicodemos the Hagiorite) categories or kinds of saints, namely, Apostles, Martyrs, Prophets, Hierarchs, and Ascetic Saints *(Hosioi)*, plus the Righteous *(Dikaioi)*. Though the categories Teachers and Confessors are possible, they are generally subsumed under one of the six categories listed. Each of the categories represents a way of becoming a saint. *Askesis* — spiritual endeavor or training — is necessary. *Askesis* involves bodily and mental practices. Professor Cavarnos discusses fasting, vigils, standing, prostrations, and silence in connection with bodily practices; and repentance, concentration, meditation, inner attention, and prayer in connection with mental practices. Using the Greek Church Fathers to support his assertions, he points out that man cannot attain perfect purity without the help of Divine grace. It is through Divine grace that a radical purification of the inner man is effected. He quotes Saint Seraphim of Sarov to stress the particular role of prayer: "Of course, every good work done for the sake of Christ gives us the grace of the Holy Spirit, but prayer provides it most of all, for prayer is, as it were, always at hand as an instrument for the acquisition of the grace of the Spirit . . . , and its practice is available to everyone" (pp. 44-45).

Prayer unites man with God. Dr. Cavarnos concludes with an eloquent quotation from Nicodemos the Hagiorite regarding this union:"From union with God is born the discrimination of truth from falsehood; the perception of the hidden mysteries of nature; foresight and foreknowledge of things; Divine effulgence; illumination of the heart; the amazing and ecstatic love of God by all the powers of the soul; being caught up to the Lord; the revelation of the insoluble mysteries of God. In a word, from this union is born the *theosis* of man, which is longed for by all . . . and is the final end and purpose, God's foremost and highest goal" (pp. 139-140).

Ways and Means to Sanctity, though brief and compact, is a rich source for identifying the essence of Orthodox Christian teaching.

14

*THE FUTURE LIFE ACCORDING TO ORTHODOX TEACHING**

Cavarnos' work, *The Future Life According to Orthodox Teaching (He Mellousa Zoe kata ten Orthodoxon Didaskalian)*, was originally inspired by a talk that he gave on the subject of the after-life at the invitation of the New England Clergy Brotherhood of St. Andrew on January 28, 1982, in Boston. He was moved to revise and enlarge it in book form for a wider audience because of the ever growing interest in the after-life, much of this interest having been spurred by the medical profession, which has its own clinical definitions of death and which has done some startling reviving of patients who were "clinically dead." So, the question of life after life, as some now put it, has greater relevance today than ever.

In his brief exposition, he endeavors to present an outline of the Orthodox Christian view on the future life by examining the Scriptures, the Church Fathers, and other Orthodox sources. He appends to his own analysis the pertinent passages on the soul from Jesus, Basil the Great, Gregory the Theologian, Macarios the Egyptian, John Damascene, Symeon the New Theologian, Gregory Palamas; on the continued life of the soul after death from Ecclesiastes, the Wisdom of Solomon, the Gospel according to Luke, the Acts of the Apostles, the Epistles to the Corinthians and Hebrews, the Epistle of Peter, and the

---

*Review published in *The Hellenic Chronicle,* March 29, 1984.

ΚΩΝΣΤΑΝΤΙΝΟΥ Π. ΚΑΒΑΡΝΟΥ
ΚΑΘΗΓΗΤΟΥ ΠΑΝΕΠΙΣΤΗΜΙΟΥ

Η ΜΕΛΛΟΥΣΑ ΖΩΗ ΚΑΤΑ ΤΗΝ ΟΡΘΟΔΟΞΟΝ ΔΙΔΑΣΚΑΛΙΑΝ

ΕΚΔΟΣΕΙΣ
"ΟΡΘΟΔΟΞΟΥ ΤΥΠΟΥ,,
ΑΘΗΝΑΙ 1984

Revelation of John, and from the Church Fathers: the unknown author of the Epistle to Diognetos, Justin the Philosopher, Antony the Great, Macarios the Egyptian, Athanasios the Great, Basil the Great, Gregory the Theologian, John Chrysostom, Mark the Ascetic, Abba Dorotheos, John Climacos, John Damascene, Symeon the New Theologian, Niketas Stethatos, Gregory Palamas, Cosmas Aitolos, Athanasios Parios, Nicodemos the Hagiorite, and Nectarios of Aegina. Dr. Cavarnos also includes hymnography concerning the immortality of the soul, and Scriptural passages regarding the resurrection of the dead and the Second Coming from the Psalms of David, Isaiah, Ezekiel, Daniel, the Gospel according to Matthew, the First Epistle to the Corinthians, and the Revelation of John. The notes and bibliography provide additional material for those wishing to probe further. The book is a handy compendium of the teachings of the Orthodox Church on the after-life and, of course, is centered on the Orthodox belief in the immortality of the soul.

For the Orthodox Christian, death does not constitute annihilation of the human existence: there is a continuation of the human soul, apart from the body. The Orthodox believe that the soul, even when separated from the body, continues to possess self-consciousness, to think with clarity and to possess feeling. It is also believed that after death the soul retains an integral memory, remembering everything, and possesses sensations that correspond to the bodily sensations of sight and hearing. Cavarnos sees these beliefs reinforced by contemporary medical science.

An "inner" and an "outer" human being constitute what we describe as a human being. Dr. Cavarnos argues that though medical science is concerned with the restoration of human health and the preservation of human life, it is religion that goes beyond this to deal with metaphysical and ethical problems, and that the Orthodox Church, basing its teachings on Holy Scripture and the Fathers, has the fullest and truest teaching on the subjects of the constitution of human beings, the nature of the soul, the relation of the soul to the body, the nature of death, paradise and hell, and the destiny of man in general. The Church concerns itself with the whole man – physical and spiritual – and her teachings are contained in Scripture, in the writings of the Fathers and doctors of the Church, especially the ascetics and mystics, in the lives of the saints, in church hymody and iconography.

Dr. Cavarnos is careful to describe the Orthodox position on the Middle Condition – the condition of souls between death and the general Resurrection – in which souls have a foretaste of their future. Complete blessedness and complete damnation come after the Second Coming of Christ and the so-called General Judgment. Paradise and hell are shown to be characterized by levels and topographically. When the bodies are resurrected as spiritual bodies, then the General and Final Judgment will take place, with the blessedness and glory of the righteous souls becoming more complete and the damnation of the sinful souls becoming final. In both cases, the souls will be reunited with their bodies, changed into spiritual ones, insusceptible of corruption and death.

The Future Life According to Orthodox Teaching provides the committed Orthodox Christian and the inquisitive non-Orthodox with a clear, succinct, and more than adequately documented treatment of the subject that should command the attention of every serious Christian.

PART III

MODERN ORTHODOX SAINTS

MODERN ORTHODOX SAINTS

1

ST. COSMAS AITOLOS

Great Missionary, Awakener, Illuminator, and holy Martyr of Greece. An account of his Life, Character and Message, including his teaching on God, Heaven and Hell, and his Prophecies, together with Selections from his Sermons.

By
CONSTANTINE CAVARNOS

Third Edition
Revised and considerably enlarged

INSTITUTE FOR BYZANTINE
AND MODERN GREEK STUDIES
115 Gilbert Road
Belmont, Massachusetts 02178
U.S.A.

1
ST. COSMAS AITOLOS*

In 1971, Constantine Cavarnos embarked on a truly significant project, a series of books on modern Eastern Orthodox saints that will include Macarios of Corinth (1731-1805), Nicodemos the Hagiorite (1749-1809), Seraphim of Sarov (1759-1833), and Nectarios of Aegina (1846-1920). The first to be published in this series is *St. Cosmas Aitolos* (1714-1779), who was officially declared a saint by the Ecumenical Patriarchate of Constantinople on April 20, 1961. Dr. Cavarnos describes him as "undoubtedly the greatest missionary of modern Greece" and "the Father of the modern Greek nation," a man who "played a role of supreme importance in the moral and religious awakening and enlightenment of the Greeks during the second half of the eighteenth century, and thus more than anyone else inaugurated the modern Greek era" (p. 11). Cosmas Aitolos has also been described as "the Missionary of the Balkans," because his work and influence extended to Constantinople, Albania, and south Serbia, as well as Greece. The *Analytic Bibliography of Cosmas Aitolos* (1765-1967) by Kostas Sardelis lists more than thirty books and six hundred articles on Aitolos, surely concrete evidence of his importance.

---

*Review published in *St. Vladimir's Theological Quarterly*, Vol. 16, No. 1, 1972, pp. 45-46.

ST. COSMAS AITOLOS
Panel icon.

Cavarnos has felt that an introduction to the spirituality of such men as St. Cosmas Aitolos needs to be made available in a convenient, inexpensive format, and has admirably inaugurated the series by providing the reader with an introductory essay on the main features of the saint's life, character, and teaching (revised and expanded from an article that originally appeared in *St. Vladimir's Seminary Quarterly* 10.4, 1966), with a translation of "The Life of Saint Cosmas" by his disciple Sapphiros Christodoulidis, and selected passages from his teaching on such subjects as God, love, humility, confession, fasting, virginity, women, death, and Scripture. A section of notes provides additional information and sources. The book itself is typographically a pleasure to work with and handsome in its simplicity.

Professor Cavarnos has commendably inaugurated a series that will be invaluable for an informed understanding of modern Orthodox spirituality.

MODERN ORTHODOX SAINTS

2

ST. MACARIOS OF CORINTH

Archbishop of Corinth, Guardian of Sacred Tradition, Reviver of Orthodox Mysticism, Compiler of the *Philokalia*, Spiritual Striver, Enlightener and Guide, and Trainer of Martyrs. An account of his Life, Character and Message, together with selections from three of his Publications

By
CONSTANTINE CAVARNOS

INSTITUTE FOR BYZANTINE
AND MODERN GREEK STUDIES
115 Gilbert Road
Belmont, Massachusetts 02178
U.S.A.

2
ST. MACARIOS OF CORINTH*

For those who might wonder whether there are or can be any saints in the modern world, the project undertaken by Constantine Cavarnos on modern Orthodox saints will certainly stand as concrete testimony of the presence and influence of a select number of holy men in the contemporary world. In the first volume of this series he published his *St. Cosmas Aitolos* (1971), an account of the life (1714-1779), character, and message of a missionary, illuminator and martyr of Greece, together with selections from his teachings. In this volume on Cosmas' younger contemporary (1731-1805), Dr. Cavarnos follows much the same format as in the previous book, that is, an introductory chapter on the saint's life, character, and contributions; an annotated translation of the life of the Saint by his close friend Athanasios Parios; the latter's account of some miracles of St. Macarios; and translations of passages selected from his three most important publications, namely, *Concerning Continual Communion, New Martyrologium,* and *Philokalia,* as well as an annotated list of the saint's writings.

This kind of book is valuable for the contemporary student of Orthodox Christianity, particularly its creative monastic aspect. As Professor Cavarnos emphasizes, "St. Macarios was not only a great reformer of the Church,

---

*Review published in *St. Vladimir's Theological Quarterly,* Vol. 21, No. 1, 1977, p. 56.

St. Macarios of Corinth

an inspirer, an enlightener, a helper and spiritual guide of men, but also a great ascetic, who strove to perfect himself and attain union with God" (p. 39). A beloved Archbishop of Corinth, a guardian of sacred Tradition, a reviver of Orthodox mysticism, compiler of the very important *Philokalia,* a teacher and trainer of martyrs, St. Macarios is a modern Orthodox saint with whose life and works every Orthodox Christian should be familiar, and from which every Christian could derive inspiration and spiritual sustenance.

MODERN ORTHODOX SAINTS

3

ST. NICODEMOS
THE HAGIORITE

Great Theologian and Teacher of the Orthodox Church, Reviver of Hesychasm, Moralist, Canonist, Hagiologist, and writer of Liturgical Poetry. An account of his Life, Character and Message, together with a Comprehensive List of his Writings and Selections from them

By

CONSTANTINE CAVARNOS

INSTITUTE FOR BYZANTINE
AND MODERN GREEK STUDIES
115 Gilbert Road
Belmont, Massachusetts 02178
U.S.A.

3

ST. NICODEMOS THE HAGIORITE*

In 1955, the Ecumenical Patriarchate of Constantinople officially recognized the sainthood of St. Nicodemos the Hagiorite (1749-1809) for his great contributions to the Church in theology, in his exemplary Christian mode of life, his virtues, and his holiness, even though he had been so regarded unofficially long before this: "During his entire holy life he had only one care and concern, to serve the Divine Will and to benefit his neighbor" (p. 92).

His entire life was spent in spiritual *askesis,* and he is regarded by many as "one of the greatest theologians of the post-Byzantine period, and the greatest of all those who led a monastic life on the Holy Mountain from the beginning to this day" (p. 58). There can be no doubt that Nicodemos was an extraordinary religious writer, contributing significantly to ascetical-mystical theology, ethics, canon law, exegesis, hagiology, liturgics, and hymnography. His writings in these fields show, according to Dr. Cavarnos, "not only depth, historical and exegetical accuracy, fidelity to the Orthodox Tradition, extraordinary erudition, real literary gifts and a very strong desire to edify, but also remarkable many-sidedness" (p. 57). However, Nicodemos was by no means an academic theo-

---

*Review published in *The Greek Orthodox Theological Review,* Vol. XIX, No.2, Autumn 1974, pp. 216-217.

ST. NICODEMOS THE HAGIORITE

St. Nicodemos the Hagiorite

logical scholar, but a very powerful spiritual guide and personal counselor, whose influence has been widely felt throughout the Orthodox world. It is no wonder that Professor Cavarnos has been inspired to continue his impressive series on *Modern Orthodox Saints* (inaugurated in 1971) by dedicating this volume to the important figure of Nicodemos. The format of the previous volumes is followed, in that Cavarnos himself provides a never previously published lengthy introductory chapter (pp. 11-63) on the life, works, concerns, and evaluative assessment of Saint Nicodemos, a list of "Works of the Saint" (pp. 96-114), available for the first time in English, and the most complete and up-to-date bibliography of the saint, as well as a translation of the "Life of Saint Nicodemos" (pp. 64-95) by the monk Gerasimos Micragiannanitis of the Holy Mountain of Athos. The original of the "Life" was first published on Athos in 1955 and appeared as part of the *Akolouthia* in honor of the saint. Dr. Cavarnos has made this particular *vita* available because it is more comprehensive and more elegant than others that could have been translated. The "Selected Passages from the Works of St. Nicodemos" (pp. 115-145) give the reader a valuable selection of passages that are particularly characteristic of his teaching and that are especially related and relevant to concerns of contemporary persons interested in Orthodox spirituality. Among the subjects noted are man's dual nature, the soul, the destiny of the soul after death, the Resurrection, spiritual food, Divine Scripture, Church Fathers, the Holy Canons, reading, chanting, sin, conscience, Paradise, the way to *theosis*, and the Jesus Prayer.

Perhaps the best summary of St. Nicodemos's life and activity is his own statement that "The greatest and most perfect achievement that man can think of is to approach God and be united with Him" (p. 131). Dr. Cavarnos continues to deserve high praise for making available to the English-reading public extremely valuable compact volumes on modern Orthodox saints that inspiringly reveal their Christian spirituality to the contemporary world.

4

ST. NIKEPHOROS OF CHIOS*

The present volume follows pretty much the format of the three previous volumes of the series *Modern Orthodox Saints.* Dr. Cavarnos contributes an introduction (pp. 11- 46) that provides basic information on the life, character, and teachings of St. Nikephoros of Chios and an assessment of him as writer of sacred poetry and lives of saints, educator, spiritual striver and trainer of martyrs. "The Life of St. Nikephoros by Emily Sarou" (pp. 47-64), which is here translated into English, constitutes the second chapter. Emily Sarou was the daughter of the prominent Chian historiographer and educator George I. Zolotas, and her biography of the saint was first published in Chios in 1907. The "Works of the Saint" (pp. 65-75) is the first comprehensive list to be published and comprises the third chapter. The fourth and fifth chapters respectively are "Selected Passages from the Prose Works of the Saint" (pp. 76-80) and "Anthology from the Poetry of the Saint" (pp. 81-90). They have been compiled "with a view to giving some of the most representative, instructive, and uplifting selections from his writings." There are notes (pp. 91-98) for the reader who would like to probe more deeply, and an appendix of "Brief Biographies" (pp. 99-110) of eleven modern martyrs and other Orthodox saints who are treated in St. Nikephoros' works and men-

---

*Review, published in *The Greek Orthodox Theological Review,* Vol. XXII, No. 2, Summer 1977, p. 236.

MODERN ORTHODOX SAINTS

4

ST. NIKEPHOROS OF CHIOS

Outstanding Writer of Liturgical Poetry and Lives of Saints, Educator, Spiritual Striver, and Trainer of Martyrs. An account of his Life, Character and Message, together with a Comprehensive List of his Publications, Selections from them, and Brief Biographies of eleven Neomartyrs and other Orthodox Saints who are treated in his works

By

CONSTANTINE CAVARNOS

INSTITUTE FOR BYZANTINE
AND MODERN GREEK STUDIES
115 Gilbert Road
Belmont, Massachusetts 02178
U.S.A.

St. Nikephoros of Chios

tioned in this volume. A preface, selected bibliography, and index complete this work, which for the first time makes available in English a book dealing with St. Nikephoros.

St. Nikephoros of Chios will be of interest to students of the cultural and religious history of Greece during the period of Turkish rule *(Tourkotratia)*, as well as to those interested in Orthodox Christian spirituality. Consistently Orthodox, St. Nikephoros presents as a main thrust the development of the virtues whereby man achieves likeness to God, through wich is attained *theosis* (deification), union with God, participation in God's perfection and glory. Blessedness through grace is viewed as man's highest goal and one that characterized the lives of the saints. Though St. Nikephoros never left Chios, his influence and reputation were widespread in the Greek Orthodox world and continue to provide spiritual inspiration and illumination to countless Christians of the Orthodox faith.

5

ST. SERAPHIM OF SAROV*

"He was a spiritual striver, a man of prayer, a mystic who attained the goal of Christian life as he described it: the possession of the grace of the Holy Spirit. He sought not only his own good, but also the good of others, having served as a teacher of monks, a protector and spiritual guide of nuns, a healer and counselor of an immense number of people. His life as he lived it shone and continues to shine. It guided those who came to him during his ministry and countless others in the generations that followed, and serves as a great beacon in our own age" (p. 92).

With the above words does Professor Mary-Barbara Zeldin of Hollins College, Virginia, and editor of the book *Peter Yakovelevich Chaadayev* and co-editor of a three-volume *Russian Philosophy,* conclude her extensive chapter (pp. 48-92) on one of the most popular of modern Orthodox saints, St. Seraphim of Sarov (1759-1833), before she presents us with her crystal-clear translations of *A Conversation with the Saint by Nicholas A. Motovilov (ca.* 1831) and *Spiritual Counsels* (written in 1839 — six years after the repose of the saint). This was a saint who never wrote down anything himself, who "saw the image of God in every man, and the sight filled him with joy" (p. 57), a *starets (geron),* whose memory is celebrated by the

---

*Review published in *St. Vladimir's Theological Quarterly,* Vol. 25, No. 2, 1981, pp. 138-139.

MODERN ORTHODOX SAINTS

5

ST. SERAPHIM OF SAROV

Widely beloved Mystic, Healer, Comforter, and Spiritual Guide. An account of his Life, Character and Message, together with a very edifying Conversation with his disciple Motovilov on the acquisition of the Grace of the Holy Spirit, and the Saint's Spiritual Counsels.

By

CONSTANTINE CAVARNOS

and

MARY-BARBARA ZELDIN

INSTITUTE FOR BYZANTINE
AND MODERN GREEK STUDIES
115 Gilbert Road
Belmont, Massachusetts 02178
U.S.A.

Russian Orthodox Church on January 2, the day of his repose, and with special services on July 19.

The *St. Seraphim of Sarov* volume presents the reader with a full account of the life, character and message of the saint, and is the first volume to appear in this series devoted to a non-Greek saint. The publication of the Greek volumes was motivated, to a great extent, by the unavailability or limited availability of information about modern Greek saints. The current volume does not have the same genesis, since a number of good and useful publications about St. Seraphim are currently available in English. However, these give only partial treatment of the subject. The present volume "offers a detailed account of St. Seraphim's life and teaching, and in addition a substantial introduction to both, placing them in the context of the long tradition of Orthodox monastic spirituality" (p. vii).

Dr. Cavarnos makes his distinct contribution to this book with the long Introduction (pp. 13-47), in which he gives us some fundamental biographical information about the man who at Baptism was named Prokhor, and was the son of Isidore and Agatha Moshnin. He counters those observers who find the saint odd or unique within traditional Orthodoxy. Thus he states that "When carefully related to the long Orthodox tradition of monasticism, the facts about St. Seraphim show him to have been an authentic follower of it, one who never abandoned this tradition, and always stood within the borders of Orthodoxy in general" (p. 28). And he places him within the Athonite tradition of *hesychasm,* pointing to his practices in fasting, vigils, frequent Holy Communion, mental prayer, standing during church services and during private prayer, confinement ("enclosure"), and silence. Even his special

St. Seraphim of Sarov

St. Seraphim of Sarov 147

devotion to the Theotokos is shown to have precedents in Athonite monasticism in particular. Professor Cavarnos draws parallels with a number of other Orthodox saints and with monastic practices on Mount Athos and in Orthodox monasticism in general.

Clearly enunciated in *A Conversation* is, he notes, the idea that man's highest goal is *theosis,* union with God through grace. God is the Creator, the Almighty, the Ruler of All, the Trinity. Grace is acquired through the sacraments of Holy Baptism, Chrismation and Communion, through prayer, vigils, fasting, almsgiving, and other virtues. In *Spiritual Counsels* God, the virtues of hope, love, patience, humility, care of the soul, the practices of fasting, silence, guarding of the heart, and prayer are discussed. Dr. Cavarnos is quick to point out that there is nothing here that cannot be found in the *Philokalia* and other works of the great ascetical-mystical Fathers of the Orthodox Church.

Professor Zeldin points out that this Christian saint was and is especially revered by Russians because his teaching spread to all parts of Russia and was responsible for initiating a new religious consciousness in an age of growing materialism; he appears as the embodiment of all that is meant by Russian spirituality; and that his life seems to synthesize all the ways by which a soul can rise to God.

Even today the Christian can turn to *A Conversation with the Saint by Nicholas A. Motovilov* for guidance on the goal of a Christian life and to *Spiritual Counsels of the Saint* for wisdom on God, hope, love for God, the preservation of truths one has come to know, talkativeness, prayer, sorrow, despondency, patience and humility, care of the soul, provision of the soul, peace of the soul, preservation of the peace of the soul, guarding the heart, recognizing the movement of the heart, ascetic progress, fasting, solitude and silence, the active and contemplative life, the eremetic life, and instructions to a novice.

This successful joint textual effort, supported by notes, a good bibliography, and an index, will provide students and faithful with an excellent comprehensive view of one of Orthodox Christianity's most illustrious saints.

SAROV MONASTERY

6

ST. ARSENIOS OF PAROS*

In volume 6 of *Modern Orthodox Saints*, devoted to St. Arsenios of Paros, Cavarnos follows the pattern that he has already established for the previous volumes. He provides a preface and a substantial introduction to the saint, reproduces in translation the life of the saint from his Greek biographer (in this case by the Abbot of the Monastery of Longovarda on the island of Paros for more than half a century, Philotheos Zervakos), provides in English translation accounts of fourteen miracles of St. Arsenios, given by Father Zervakos, and some spiritual counsels of the saint, plus notes, a bibliography and an index.

This is the first book in any language other than Greek to be published on St. Arsenios (1800-1877), a younger contemporary of St. Nikephoros of Chios and St. Seraphim of Sarov. Dr. Cavarnos sees St. Arsenios as a remarkable confessor, spiritual guide, educator, ascetic, miracle-worker, and healer who spent his last thirty-seven years on the island of Paros, and seeks to reveal this saint's life, character and thought to a wider public. The book should also be helpful in offering a better understanding of the Kollyvades Movement and its influence far beyond Mount Athos, its place of origin, and of his Elder, Father Daniel of Zagora, who also belonged to it. In 1967 the Ecumenical

---

*Review published in *The Greek Orthodox Theological Review*, Vol. XXIV, No. 1, Spring 1979, p. 78.

MODERN ORTHODOX SAINTS

6

ST. ARSENIOS OF PAROS

Remarkable Confessor, Spiritual Guide, Educator, Ascetic, Miracle-Worker, and Healer. An account of his Life, Character, Message and Miracles

By
CONSTANTINE CAVARNOS

INSTITUTE FOR BYZANTINE
AND MODERN GREEK STUDIES
115 Gilbert Road
Belmont, Massachusetts 02178
U.S.A.

St. Arsenios of Paros

Patriarchate of Constantinople recognized Arsenios of Paros as a saint of the Orthodox Church.

In preparing this volume, Cavarnos has made extensive use of *The Life, Conduct and Miracles of Our Father Arsenios the New, Who Led a Life of Spiritual Endeavor on the Island of Paros* by Archimandrite Philotheos Zervakos. In addition, he has culled necessary information from a variety of primary and secondary sources listed in his bibliography.

One of St. Arsenios' own admonitions could probably be used to summarize his own life, work, and counsel to all Christians:

"Be at peace with others, have humility, remember Christ and imitate His humility, obedience, and love for all – without which you cannot be saved, without which the other virtues are of no avail" (p. 105).

7
ST. NECTARIOS OF AEGINA

St. Nectarios of Aegina, the seventh volume of the series *Modern Orthodox Saints,* is dedicated to the most recent officially recognized saint of Greece, Nectarios Kephalas, Metropolitan of Pentapolis (1846-1920), who founded the Holy Trinity Convent on the island of Aegina, where he lived a monastic life from 1908 to 1920. In this book, Dr. Cavarnos seeks "to give an account, not only of St. Nectarios' life and some of his miracles, but also of the nature and scope of the more than thirty books and the many pamphlets and articles which he published" (p. vii). In addition, he presents an extensive anthology from them on diverse topics, and an essay in which he highlights and summarizes the saint's important teaching about God. His effort is one that began twenty years ago and contributed to his becoming more and more knowledgeable about the life, character and thought of St. Nectarios of Aegina. The present volume constitutes the first on this saint to be published in English, or in any language other than Greek. Though more than a dozen books on St. Nectarios have circulated in Greek, they can be generally characterized as biographical, laudatory and concerned primarily with his miracles. His reputation as a miracle-worker, particularly as a healer of every kind of disease, no doubt contributed to this emphasis. But Dr. Cavarnos points out

---
*Review published in *St. Vladimir's Theological Quarterly,* Vol. 25, No. 3, 1981, pp. 209-210.

MODERN ORTHODOX SAINTS

7

ST. NECTARIOS OF AEGINA

Metropolitan of Pentapolis, great Theologian, Philosopher, Moralist, Educator, Ascetic, Mystic, Miracle-Worker and Healer. An account of his Life, Character, Message and Miracles, together with a Comprehensive List of his Writings, Selections from them, and an Essay on his teaching on God.

By

CONSTANTINE CAVARNOS

INSTITUTE FOR BYZANTINE
AND MODERN GREEK STUDIES
115 Gilbert Road
Belmont, Massachusetts 02178
U.S.A.

St. Nectarios of Aegina 155

that St. Nectarios was a prolific writer, theologian, philosopher, moralist, educator, poet, ascetic and mystic. As the most widely known Greek Orthodox saint after Sts. Cosmas Aitolos and Nicodemos the Hagiorite, according to Dr. Cavarnos, "The extent and character of the writings of St. Nectarios place him among the great educators, moralists and religious philosophers of modern Greece, and among the holy Fathers and Teachers of the Orthodox Church" (p. 74).

The St. Nectarios volume is organized in much the same way as the previous volumes. The apolytikion, kontakion and megalynarion of the saint precede the main body of the work. After the Preface, there is an extensive and illuminating introduction by the author (pp. 11-85); a translation of "The Life of St. Nectarios" by his student and friend Joachim Spetsieris (pp. 86-104); "Miracles of the Saint," including personal testimonials from people who were cured by him (pp. 105-116); "Works of the Saint" — an impressive bibliography of books authored, books edited, books put into verse, pamphlets, articles, letters and unpublished works (pp. 117-129); a substantial essay "On God" by Dr. Cavarnos, which includes citations from St. Nectarios (pp. 130-153); "Selected Passages from the Writings of the Saint" (pp. 154-187); "Notes" (pp. 188-205); "Bibliography," practically all in Greek (pp. 206-210); and an index.

Dr. Cavarnos' book gives us a very clear picture of the saint. Especially clear is how so much of St. Nectarios' life, work and thought are characterized by his love of God. As he, himself said: "Love of God is knowledge of God, for one who loves, loves what one has come to know, and it is impossible for one to love what is unknown .... Love of God expresses the yearning to be united with God as

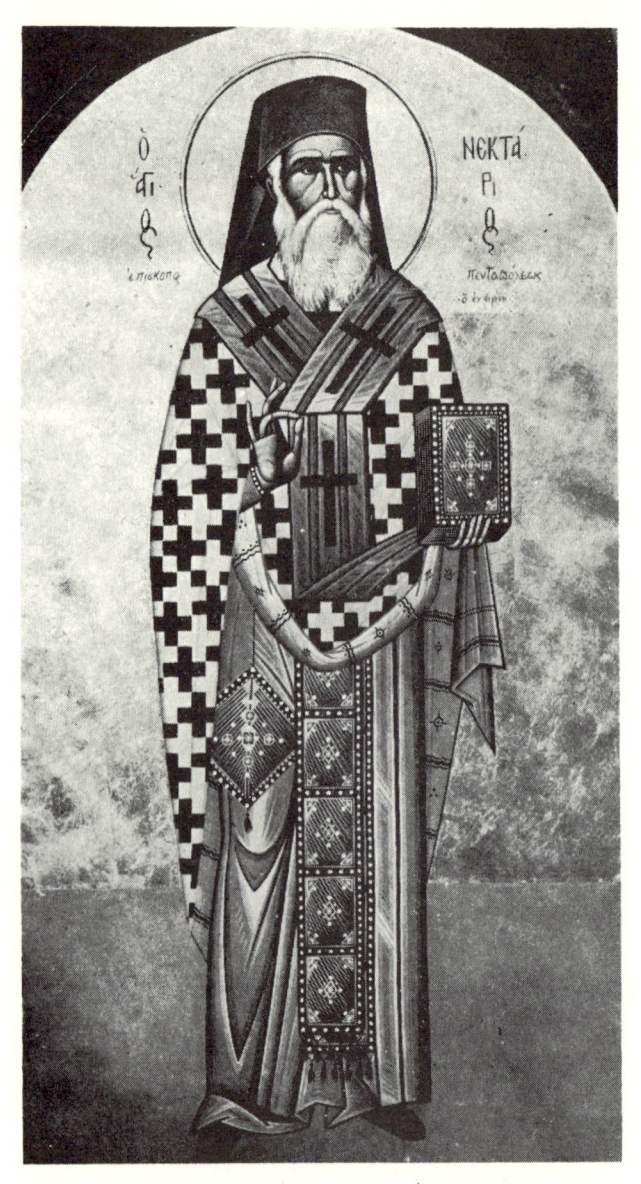

St. Nectarios of Aegina

the supreme good" (p. 177). St. Nectarios' life and conduct is eloquently characterized in the following passage: "His whole life was nothing else that a continuous doxology to God, and a tireless effort and assiduous concern to benefit suffering society morally and religiously. He lived *in* the world, but was *not,* as the Savior says, *of* the world. He trod on the earth, yet conducted himself like a citizen of heaven. He had the form of a man, but lived like an angel. He was clothed with flesh, but was a strict keeper and guardian of chastity. He associated with various kinds of persons, but spoke as a spiritual man, alien to the present world. He was transported by sublime ideals and warmed by the aspiration for moral perfection; and hence he abided in a state of inner calm and blessedness. His was a peace-making holiness, inspired by evangelical virtue and meditation on the eternal Kingdom of God" (p. 104).

St. Nectarios of Aegina is a splendid addition to the volumes in the *Modern Orthodox Saints* series. It deserves to be in the library of every Orthodox Christian and of every institution concerned with or interested in the history, work and thought of the Orthodox Church. It shows that Orthodox spirituality is still at work in the modern world.

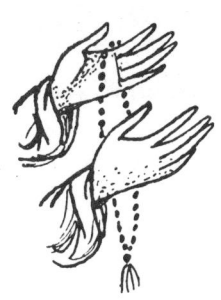

MODERN ORTHODOX SAINTS

8

ST. SAVVAS THE NEW

Remarkable Ascetic, Confessor, Spiritual Guide, Iconographer, Miracle-Worker and Healer (1862-1948). An account of his Life, Character, Message, Miracles and Icons, together with his nine Definitions of Irreproachable Monastic Conduct.

By
CONSTANTINE CAVARNOS

INSTITUTE FOR BYZANTINE
AND MODERN GREEK STUDIES
115 Gilbert Road
Belmont, Massachusetts 02178
U.S.A.

8
ST. SAVVAS THE NEW*

Continuing the unique series *Modern Orthodox Saints* that he began in 1971 with *St. Cosmas Aitolos,* Constantine Cavarnos recently produced an eighth volume, devoted to *St. Savvas the New,* who flourished on the island of Kalymnos and is Greece's most recent saint. The series is remarkable for systematically bringing to the English-reading public basic information on modern saints that is simply not readily available elsewhere.

Two books appeared on St. Savvas the New (1862-1948), the patron, saint of Kalymnos − both in Greek − prior to the publication of Cavarnos' book. This work contains a substantial introduction, which he calls "Introductory" (pp. 15-59); a translation of "The Life of St. Savvas the New by Vasilios Papanikolaou" (pp. 61-82); "Miracles of the Saint" (pp. 83-95); and an illustrated survey of "The Icons of the Saint" (pp. 97-119). It also contains a translation and discussion of St. Savvas' "Definitions of Irreproachable Monastic Conduct" (pp. 120-127); quotations on the "Value of Reading Lives of Saints," twenty-three illustrations, notes, a selected bibliography and index. In his long "Introductory," Dr. Cavarnos provides the reader with a "consistent, continuous and comprehensive account of St. Savvas' life, conduct, character, work and influence" (p. ix), to cite his own words. Here, and in "The Life of St. Savvas

---
*From a review forthcoming in *Church and Theology* (London).

the New" that follows, we are made to feel the personal presence of a monastic who had spent time on the Holy Mountain of Athos, the Holy Land, the island of Aegina, and the island of Kalymnos.

When one reads about the unpretentious life of this latest Orthodox saint, whose education was extremely limited, who became an unusual ascetic, confessor, iconographer, miracle-worker and healer, one cannot help but be impressed by the extent of his Christian charity and humility. Though he left many icons, he authored no books and no pamphlets – only a two-page text in his own handwriting called *Definitions of Irreproachable Monastic Conduct*. Though no scholar, he read sacred books like the *Gospels*, the *Psalter*, the *Ladder of Divine Ascent* of St. John Climacos, *Evergetinos,* and the *Philokalia*. He was a man of incessant prayer and worship who practiced self-restraint and strove for inner, spiritual development. He did not engage in abstruse theological investigations and renounced all material possessions. At the same time he reached out to help all those in need about him. In his "Life," Vasilios Papanikolaou puts it this way:

"His life was a long state of holy obedience. He saw obedience linked with blessed humility. Of course, one may say that God's commandments are reducible to one: love. When one loves God, he obeys. When he obeys, he humbles himself" (p. 77).

So great then was St. Savvas' love of God and submission to His will, and his love of man, that he dedicated all his life to serving Him and his fellow man.

Cavarnos' *St. Savvas the New* shows how a profoundly God-centered man can justifiably come to be regarded as a saint, to be greatly admired and even emulated.

St. Savvas the New
Panel icon. 1961. Convent of All Saints, Kalymnos.
By Michael Kafsokalyvitis, Mount Athos.

BIBLIOGRAPHY

WORKS BY CONSTANTINE CAVARNOS

I. Books

(1) *A Dialogue between Bergson, Aristotle, and Philologos*. Preface by Professor John D. Wild of Harvard University. First Bowdoin Prize, 1947, Harvard University. Cambridge, Massachusetts, 1949. Pp. 60. 2nd edition, containing two pages of comments on the *Dialogue* by Harvard Professors Clarence Irving Lewis and Raphael Demos, Belmont, Massachusetts, Institute for Byzantine and Modern Greek Studies, 1973. Pp. 62.

(2) *Byzantine Sacred Music*. Belmont, Mass., Institute for Byzantine and Modern Greek Studies, 1956. Pp. 31. Reprinted 1966, 1974, 1981.

(3) *Byzantine Sacred Art*. Subtitle: *Selected writings of the contemporary Greek icon painter Fotis Kontoglous on the Sacred Arts according to the Tradition of Eastern Orthodox Christianity, compiled, translated from the Greek, and edited with a preface, introduction, notes and illustrations by Constantine Cavarnos*. New York, Vantage Press, 1957. Pp. 111 + 11 plates. 2nd, revised and considerably enlarged, edition, Belmont, Mass., Institute for Byzantine and Modern Greek Studies, 1985. Pp. 171, 25 illus.

(4) *Orthodoxy in America (He Orthodoxia sten Amerike)*. Athens, 1958. Pp. 31.

(5) *Anchored in God.* Subtitle: *An inside account of life, art, and thought on the Holy Mountain of Athos.* Athens, "Astir" Publishing Co., 1959. Pp. 230, 74 illus. and map. 2nd edition, Belmont, Mass., Institute for Byzantine and Modern Greek Studies, 1975.

(6) *Man and the Universe in American Philosophy (To Sympan kai ho Anthropos sten Amerikanike Philosophia).* Athens, "Astir" Publishing Co., 1959. Pp. 120 + 3 plates.

(7) *Symbols and Proofs of Immortality (Athanatou Zoes Symbola kai Endeixeis).* Athens, "Astir" Publishing Co., 1964. Pp. 200, 40 illus.

(8) *The Question of the Union of the Two Churches (To Zetema tes Henoseos ton Dyo Ekklesion).* With a Prologue and illustrations by Photios Kontoglou. Athens, Panhellenic Orthodox Union Editions, 1964. Pp. 32. 2nd, augmented edition, by the same publisher, 1968. Pp. 39.

(9) *Greece and Orthodoxy (Hellas kai Orthodoxia).* Athens, "Orthodox Press" Editions, 1967. Pp. 96, 2nd, revised and considerably enlarged edition, 1985.

(10) *Modern Greek Philosophers on the Human Soul.* Belmont, Mass., Institute for Byzantine and Modern Greek Studies, 1967. Pp. 111, 4 plates.

(11) *Byzantine Thought and Art.* Belmont, Mass., Institute for Byzantine and Modern Greek Studies, 1968. Pp. 139, 21 illus. 2nd edition, 1974. Reprinted 1980. Translated into Serbian by the Serbian Patriarchate and published at Belgrade, 1978. Pp. 96 of larger format, 24 illus.

(12) *Modern Greek Thought.* Belmont, Mass., Institute for Byzantine and Modern Greek Studies, 1969. Pp. 115.

Works by Constantine Cavarnos

(13) *Offering to the Convent of Evangelistria of Plomari, Lesvos (Aphieroma sto Monasteri tes Euangelistrias tou Plomariou Lesbou).* Prologue by the Metropolitan of Mytilene Iakovos. Athens, "Orthodox Press," 1970. Pp. 32, 7 illus.

(14) *The Orthodox Tradition and Modernization (He Orthodoxos Paradosis kai ho Synchronismos).* Athens, "Orthodox Press" Editions, 1971. Pp. 55, 10 illus.

(15) *Modern Orthodox Saints,* Vol. 1, *St. Cosmas Aitolos,* Belmont, Mass., Institute for Byzantine and Modern Greek Studies, 1971. Pp. 71, 1 illus. 2nd edition, 1975. 3rd, revised and augmented edition, 1985. Pp. 120, 6 illus.

(16) *Modern Orthodox Saints,* Vol. 2, *St. Macarios of Corinth.* Belmont, Mass., Institute for Byzantine and Modern Greek Studies, 1972. Pp. 118, 1 illus. 2nd edition, 1977.

(17) *The Holy Mountain.* Belmont, Mass., Institute for Byzantine and Modern Greek Studies, 1973. Pp. 172 + 16 plates. 2nd edition, 1977.

(18) *Plato's Theory of Fine Art.* Athens, "Astir" Publishing Co., 1973. Pp. 98.

(19) *Modern Orthodox Saints,* Vol. 3, *St. Nicodemos the Hagiorite.* Belmont, Mass., Institute for Byzantine and Modern Greek Studies, 1974. Pp. 167, 1 illus. 2nd edition 1979

(20) *Plato's View of Man.* Two Bowen Prize Essays (Harvard University), together with selected passages from Plato's dialogues on man and the human soul. Belmont, Mass., Institute for Byzantine and Modern Greek Studies, 1975. Pp. 95. Reprinted 1982.

(21) *The Classical Theory of Relations: A Study in the Metaphysics of Plato, Aristotle, and Thomism.* Doctoral Dissertation, revised and with a preface and indexes added. Belmont, Mass., Institute for Byzantine and Modern Greek Studies, 1975. Pp. 116.

(22) *Greek Learning and Orthodoxy (Ta Hellenika Grammata kai he Orthodoxia).* Translated from the English by Michael Marangoulas. Athens, "Orthodox Press" Editions, 1976. Pp. 48, 1 illus.

(23) *Modern Orthodox Saints,* Vol. 4, *St. Nikephoros of Chios.* Belmont, Mass., Institute for Byzantine and Modern Greek Studies, 1976. Pp. 124, 1 illus. 2nd edition, 1985.

(24) *Orthodox Iconography.* Belmont, Mass., Institute for Byzantine and Modern Greek Studies, 1977. Pp. 76 + 24 plates. Reprinted 1980.

(25) *Modern Orthodox Saints,* Vol. 6, *St. Arsenios of Paros.* Belmont, Mass., Institute for Byzantine and Modern Greek Studies, 1978. Pp. 123, 1 illus.

(26) *A Dialogue on G.E. Moore's Ethical Philosophy, together with an Account of Three Talks with G.E. Moore on Diverse Philosophical Questions.* Belmont, Mass., Institute for Byzantine and Modern Greek Studies, 1979. Pp. 68.

(27) *Philosophical Studies (Philosophika Meletemata).* Belmont, Mass., Institute for Byzantine and Modern Greek Studies, 1979. Pp. 86.

(28) *Ways and Means to Sanctity (Hodoi kai Tropoi pros ten Hagioteta).* Athens, "Orthodox Press" Editions, 1980. Pp. 55, 7 illus. 2nd edition, 1985. Pp. 71, 7 illus.

(29) *Modern Orthodox Saints,* Vol. 5, *St. Seraphim of Sarov.* With Mary-Barbara Zeldin. Belmont, Mass., Institute for Byzantine and Modern Greek Studies, 1980. Pp. 167, 1 illus. Reprinted 1984.

(30) *Modern Orthodox Saints,* Vol. 7, *St. Nectarios of Aegina.* Belmont, Mass., Institute for Byzantine and Modern Greek Studies, 1981. Pp. 222, 1 illus.

(31) *The Future Life according to Orthodox Teaching (He Mellousa Zoe kata ten Orthodoxon Didaskalian).* Athens, "Orthodox Press" Editions, 1984. Pp. 79, 2 illus. Translated into English and published by the Center for Traditionalist Orthodox Studies at Etna, Calif., 1985. Pp. 88.

(32) *The Educational Theory of Benjamin of Lesvos (He peri Paideias Theoria tou Beniamin Lesviou).* Athens, "Orthodox Press" Editions, 1984. Pp. 64, 2 illus.

(33) *Modern Orthodox Saints,* Vol. 8, *St. Savvas the New.* Belmont, Mass., Institute for Byzantine and Modern Greek Studies, 1985. Pp. 144, 23 illus.

(34) *Meetings with Kontoglou (Synanteseis me ton Kontoglou).* Athens, "Astir" Publishing Co., 1985. Pp. 224, 55 illus.

II. Pamphlets

(1) *The Icon: Its Spiritual Basis and Purpose.* Haverhill, Mass., The Byzantine Publishers, 1955. Pp. 11, 2 illus. 2nd edition, Belmont, Mass., Institute for Byzantine and Modern Greek Studies, 1973. Reprinted 1975, 1977, 1979.

(2) *Byzantine Iconography.* Translation of a text by Fotis Kontoglou. Belmont, Mass., Institute for Byzantine and Modern Greek Studies, 1956. Pp. 5.

(3) *The Rational Man According to St. Antony the Great.* Belmont, Mass., Institute for Byzantine and Modern Greek Studies, 1956. Pp. 6. Reprinted in *Orthodox Life,* Vol. 24, No. 1, January-February, 1974, Pp. 7-12.

(4) *Nicholas Berdyaev: The Meaning of the Creative Act.* A review. Belmont, Mass., Institute for Byzantine and Modern Greek Studies, 1956. Pp. 5.

(5) *Smoking and the Orthodox Christian (To Kapnisma kai ho Orthodoxos Christianos).* Excerpts from the Greek *Handbook of Counsel* and *Spiritual Exercises* of St. Nicodemos the Hagiorite, with a prologue and notes. Belmont, Mass., Institute for Byzantine and Modern Greek Studies, 1972. Pp. 15.

(6) *Saint Mark Eugenikos of Ephesus (Hagios Markos Ephesou ho Eugenikos).* Belmont, Mass., Institute for Byzantine and Modern Greek Studies, 1972. Pp. 12.

(7) *Byzantine Music (He Byzantine Mousike).* Belmont, Mass., Institute for Byzantine and Modern Greek Studies, 1978. Pp. 15.

(8) *The Relevance of Greek Letters to Orthodoxy.* New York, Greek Orthodox Archdiocese of North and South America, Department of Education, 1984. Pp. 10.

III. Selected Articles

(1) "Science and Modern Greek Thought," *The Carolina Quarterly,* Vol. IV, No. 2, March 1952, pp. 14-26.

(2) "Plato's Teaching on Fine Art," *Philosophy and Phenomenological Research*, Vol. XII, No. 4, June 1953, pp. 487-498.

(3) "Four Basic Types of Motivation in Philosophy," *The Southern Philosopher*, Vol. III, No. 2, April 1954, pp. 1-5.

(4) "The Nature and Proper Uses of Reason," *The Greek Orthodox Theological Review*, Vol. I, No. 1, August 1954, pp. 30-37.

(5) "Concerning Inner Attention," *The Greek Orthodox Theological Review*, Vol. I, No. 2, March 1955, pp. 152-159.

(6) "Orthodoxy and Tradition" ("*Orthodoxia kai Paradosis*") *Ekklesia* (Athens), September 1956, pp. 308-309.

(7) "The Metaphysics of Benjamin of Lesvos" ("*He Metaphysike tou Beniamin tou Lesbiou*"), *Lesviaka* (Mytilene), Vol. V, 1966, pp. 169-176.

(8) "Begreppet Kristen Kärlek" (The Concept of Christian Love), *Nu Och Alltid* (Stockholm), Vol. 1, Nr 1, Julen 1971, pp. 22-32.

(9) "Modern Greek Literature and the International Response to It" ("*He Neohellenike Logotechnia kai he Diethnes Autes Apechesis*"), *Epeirotike Estia* (Ioannina), November-December 1971, pp. 963-971.

(10) "Conscience as Viewed in Patristic Thought" ("*He Ennoia tes Syneideseos eis ten Pateriken Skepsin*"), *Epopteia* (Athens), 2, May 1976, pp. 28-37.

(11) "Plato's Theory of the Fine Arts" ("*Platonos Theoria ton Kalon Technon*"), *Epopteia*, 3, August 1976, pp. 38-45.

(12) *"Philokalia," Ortodoks Rost, Norsk Ortodoks Tidskrift* (Oslo), Nr. 6, December 1977, pp. 34-46.

(13) "Fine Art as Therapy According to Plato," *Philosophia* (Athens), 7, 1977, pp. 266-290; and slightly revised, in *The Personality of the Therapist*, edited by Irene Jakab, Pittsburgh, The American Society of Psychopathology of Expression, 1981, pp. 27-49.

(14) "Art as a Means of Therapy According to Aristotle," *The Classical Outlook*, Vol. LVI, No. 2, November-December 1978, pp. 25-32, Vol. LVI, No. 3, January-February 1979, pp. 56-59.

(15) "Knowing God through Icons and Hymnody," *The Greek Orthodox Theological Review*, Vol. XXIII, Nos. 3, 4, Fall/Winter 1978, pp. 282-298.

(16) "The Ways of Sanctity," *Tikhonaire* (South Canaan, Penn.), May 1979, pp. 23-30.

(17) "A Response to a Theological Apologia for the Forthcoming Great and Holy Synod," *The Greek Orthodox Theological Review*, Vol. XXIV, Nos. 2, 3, Summer/Fall 1979, pp. 123-127.

(18) "The Sacred Poetry of St. John Damascene," *Three Byzantine Sacred Poets*, edited by N.M. Vaporis, Brookline, Mass., Hellenic College Press, 1979, pp. 35-56.

(19) "The Assimilation of the Platonic Conception of the Human Soul in Byzantine Philosophico-Religious Thought," *Diotima* (Athens), Vol. 7, 1979, pp. 35-38.

(20) "Basic Elements of Aristotle's Philosophy in Byzantine Philosophico-Religious Thought," *Proceedings of the World Congress on Aristotle at Thessaloniki in 1978*, Athens, Vol. 2, 1981, pp. 11-14.

(21) "Kontoglou's General Theory of Art," *Diotima,* Vol. 9, 1981, pp. 62-66.

(22) "The Concept of Christian Love," *The Byzantine and Patristic Review,* Vol. 1, No. 1, 1982, pp. 32-43.

(23) "Saint Nicodemos the Hagiorite and the Modern Greek Enlightenment" *("Ho Hagios Nikodemos ho Hagioreites kai ho Neohellenikos Diaphotismos"), Orthodoxos Typos,* Vol. 24, Nos. 612-615, June 22, 29, July 6, 13, 1984.

(24) "Sacred and Secular Learning: the Views of the Three Great Hierarchs," *The Hellenic Chronicle,* February 14, 21, 28, March 7, 14, 1985.

IV. SELECTED REVIEWS

(1) Michelis, P.A., *An Aesthetic Examination of Byzantine Art (Aisthetike Theorese tes Byzantines Technes).* Athens, Pyrsos, 1946, pp. 220, 150 illus. *The Journal of Aesthetics and Art Criticism,* Vol. VIII, No. 4, June 1950, p. 274.

(2) Papanoutsos, E.P., *Aesthetics (Aisthetike).* Athens, Ikaros, 1948, pp. 445. *The Journal of Aesthetics and Art Criticism,* Vol. VIII, No. 4, June 1950, pp. 274-275.

(3) Theodorakopoulos, Ioannis N., *Introduction to Plato (Eisagoge ston Platona).* Athens, K. Papadogiannis, 1947, pp. 304, 2nd edition. Theodorakopoulos, I.N., *Plato's Phaedrus (Platonos Phaidros).* Athens, Adelphoi G. Rode, 1948, pp. 466. *The Classical Journal,* Vol. XLVI, No. 1, October 1950, pp. 42-44.

(4) Papanoutsos, E.P., *Ethics (Ethike).* Athens, Ikaros, 1949, pp. 453. *Krikos,* Vol. II, No. 13, October-November 1951, pp. 43-45.

(5) Michelis, P.A., *Architecture as an Art: An Applied Aesthetics (He Architektonike hos Techne: Mia Ephermosmene Aisthetike)*. Athens, Ekdoseis tou Technikou Epimeleteriou tes Hellados, 1951, pp. xvii + 364, 199 illus. *The Journal of Aesthetics and Art Criticism*, Vol. XI, No. 1, September 1952, pp. 81-82.

(6) Copleston, Frederick C., *Medieval Philosophy*, New York, Philosophical Library, 1952, pp. 194. *The Southern Philosopher*, Vol. II, No. 3, May 1953.

(7) Cavasilas, Nicholas, *The Christian Life (He Christianike Zoe)*. Athens, Brotherhood of Theologians "Zoe," 1954, pp. 106. *The Greek Orthodox Theological Review*, Vol. I, No. 2, March 1955, p. 182.

(8) Apostle, Hippocrates G., *Aristotle's Philosophy of Mathematics*. Chicago, The University of Chicago Press, 1952, pp. x + 228. *Philosophy and Phenomenological Research*, Vol. XIV. No. 3, December 1953, pp. 280-281.

(9) Papanoutsos, E.P. *La Catharsis des passions d'après Aristotle*. Athens, L'Institut Francais d'Athènes, 1953, pp. 42. *The Journal of Aesthetics and Art Criticism*, Vol. XII, No. 3, March 1954, pp. 399-400.

(10) De Magalhães-Vilhena, V., *Le Problème de Socrate: Le Socrate historique et le Socrate de Platon*. Paris, Presses Universitaires de France, 1952, pp. 568. De Magalhães-Vilhena, V., *Socrate et la légende Platonicienne*. Paris, Presses Universitaires de France, 1952, pp. 235. *Philosophy and Phenomenological Research*, Vol. XV, No. 1, September 1954, pp. 137-138.

(11) Michelis, P.A., *An Aesthetic Approach to Byzantine Art*. With a Foreword by Sir Herbert Read. London, B.T. Batsford, 1955, pp. xx + 284, 150 illus. *The Journal*

of Aesthetics and Art Criticism, Vol. XIV, No. 4, June 1956, pp. 506-507.

(12) Michelis, P.A., *The Aesthetics of Ferro-concrete Architecture (He Aisthetike tes Architektonikes tou Betonarme).* Athens, Ekdoseis tou Ethnikou Metsoviou Polytechneiou, 1955, pp. 196, 210 illus. *The Journal of Aesthetics and Art Criticism,* Vol. XVI, No. 1, September 1957, pp. 138-139.

(13) Rexine, John E., *Religion in Plato and Cicero.* New York, Philosophical Library, 1959, pp. 72. *The Classical World,* Vol. LIII, No. 5, February 1960, p. 163.

(14) Kostaras, Greg. Phil., *Martin Heidegger, the Philosopher of Care (Martin Heidegger, ho Philosophos tes Merimnes).* Athens, N. & M. Athanasopoulou, 1973, pp. 239. *Platon* (Athens), Vol. 26, Nos. 51/52, 1974, pp. 348-350.

(15) Lossky, Vladimir, *In the Image and Likeness.* New York, St. Vladimir's Press, 1975, pp. 232. *The Greek Orthodox Theological Review,* Vol. XX, Nos. 1/2, Spring-Fall 1975, pp. 85-87.

(16) Tatakis, B.N., *Byzantine Philosophy (He Byzantine Philosophia).* Athens, Hetaireia Spoudon Neohellenikou Politismou kai Genikes Paideias, 1977, pp. 380. *The Hellenic Chronicle* (Boston), May 18, 1978.

(17) Moutsopoulos, E., editor, *Philosophical Works of Petros Vraïlas-Armenis (Petrou Braïla-Armene Philosophika Erga).* Athens, Ethnikon Idryma Ereunon, 1969-1976, 5 vols., pp. 2, 209. *The Hellenic Chronicle,* April 12, 1979.

(18) Klein, Jacob, *Plato's Trilogy.* Chicago, The University of Chicago Press, 1977, pp. 200. *The Classical*

Outlook, Vol. LVII, No. 1, September-October 1979, pp. 16-17.

(19) Terzakis, Angelos, *Homage to the Tragic Muse.* Translated by Athan Anagnostopoulos. Foreword by Cedric H. Whitman. Boston, Houghton Mifflin Co., 1978, pp. 207. *The Hellenic Chronicle,* January 19, 1980.

(20) Chrysostomos, Archimandrite, *The Ancient Fathers of the Desert.* Brookline, Mass., Hellenic College Press, 1980, pp. 118. *The Greek Orthodox Theological Review,* Vol. XXVI, No. 4, Winter 1981, pp. 358-360.

(21) Piompinos, Phoivos, *Greek Iconographers down to 1821 (Hellenes Hagiographoi mechri to 1821).* Athens, 1979, pp. 339. *The Hellenic Chronicle,* August 13, 1981.

(22) Rexine, John E., *The Hellenic Spirit: Byzantine and Post Byzantine.* Belmont, Mass., Institute for Byzantine and Modern Greek Studies, 1981, pp. vi + 136. *The Hellenic Chronicle,* August 12, 1982.

(23) Maguire, Henry, *Art and Eloquence in Byzantium.* Princeton, Princeton University Press, 1981, pp. xxiii + 148. *The Greek Orthodox Theological Review,* Vol. 30, No. 1, Spring 1985, pp. 87-90

V. SELECTED TRANSLATIONS

(1) "The Ecclesiology of the Three Hierarchs," by Ioannis Karmiris, *The Greek Orthodox Theological Review,* Vol. VI, No. 2, Winter 1960-1961, pp. 135-185.

(2) "The Apostle Paul and the Unity of the Church," by Panayotis I. Bratsiotis, *The Orthodox Observer,* Vol. XXVII, No. 494, May 1961, pp. 145-149. Also published in pamphlet form together with the Greek text.

(3) "The Monastic Life in the Eastern Orthodox Church," by Panagiotis K. Christou, *The Orthodox Ethos,* by A.J. Philippou, editor, Oxford, Holywell Press Ltd., 1964, pp. 249-258.

(4) The *Philokalia,* by Sts. Macarios of Corinth and Nicodemos the Hagiorite. Cavarnos collaborated in the translation of this famous classic of Eastern Orthodox spirituality from the original Greek into English, under the editorship of G.E.H. Palmer, Philip Sherrard, and Kallistos Ware. (It is being published in five volumes in London by Faber & Faber Ltd. The first three volumes have already appeared in print.) He did the initial translation of the texts ascribed to St. Antony the Great, St. Isaiah the Solitary, Evagrios the Solitary, St. Mark the Ascetic, St. Neilos the Ascetic, St. Theodoros of Edessa, Abba Philemon, Philotheos the Sinaite, Elias Ekdikos, Symeon of Thessaloniki, and certain ones by St. Symeon the New Theologian, as well as some others.

INDEX

abstraction, 21
action, 19, 21, 56, 61, 148
aesthetics, 14, 33, 34, 36, 37, 41, 45, 62, 78, 113, 171-172
after-life, 121-124, 167
Albania, 127
America, 7, 13, 15, 16, 23-26, 33, 79-81, 108, 163
American philosophy, 14, 23-26, 27, 51, 83, 164
analysis, 14, 15, 21, 26, 37, 42, 47, 53, 119, 121
ancient Greek philosophers, 26, 27, 42, 60, 63, 67, 111
Antony the Great, 123, 168, 175
anxiety, 85
Apostle, Hippocrates G., 172
Aquinas, 53
architecture, 36, 38, 46, 77, 79, 83, 84, 95, 98, 172, 173
aretology, 61-62
aristocratic individual, 49
Aristotelianism, 51
Aristotle, 14, 18-22, 51-53, 56, 57, 60, 67, 163, 166, 170, 172
Arsenios of Paros, St., 15, 149-152, 166

art, 7, 15, 45-46, 83, 107, 164, 169, 170, 171, 174
  Byzantine, 13, 14, 29, 33, 34-39, 73-78, 81, 83, 95, 98, 103, 104, 171, 172, 174
  Western 73, 77
ascetical theology, 13, 14, 33, 37, 124
asceticism, 85, 119, 133, 135, 148
Athanasios the Great, St., 123
Athens, 23, 44, 45, 61, 62, 64, 79, 85, 89, 107, 109, 117, 164, 165, 169, 170, 171, 172, 173
Athos, Mount, 15, 77, 80-92, 104, 145, 147, 149, 160, 164, 165
attention, 66, 72, 119, 169
Augustine, St., 62

Balkans, 127
Basil the Great, 62, 90, 121, 171, 174
beauty, 45-46, 60, 62, 63, 77
  physical, 39
  spiritual, 36, 39, 46, 59, 62-63
Belgrade, 164
Benjamin of Lesvos, 14, 29, 59, 60, 64-67, 95, 167, 169
Berdyaev, 168

INDEX

Bergson, Henri, 14, 18-22, 56, 163
Bible, 67
Bowdoin Prize, 19, 163
Bowen Prize, 46, 48, 165
Bradley, F.H., 51
Bratsiotis, P.I., 174
Broad, C.D., 55, 56
Bulgaria, 75
Byzantine architecture, 77, 83, 98
Byzantine art, *see* art, Byzantine
Byzantine churches, 104
Byzantine civilization, 13, 43
Byzantine hymnography, 39, 75, 88, 89, 123, 124, 170
Byzantine iconography, 73-78, 83, 95, 98, 107, 113-116, 124, 168
Byzantine mind, 37, 38, 39, 78
Byzantine Museum, 104
Byzantine music, 14-15, 34, 36, 38-39, 70-72, 75-76, 81, 88, 89, 104, 107, 163, 168
Byzantine philosophy, 38, 42, 60, 63, 173
Byzantine studies, 26, 89
Byzantine theology, 34, 37-38
Byzantine thought, 30-39, 164, 169, 170, 174
canons of the Ecumenical Synods, 71, 109-111, 135, 137

catharsis, 172
Catholicism, Roman, 99-101
Cavasilas, Nicholas, 172
change, 19, 21
chanting, 71-72
character, 59-60
chastity, 62, 157
Christ, 34, 35, 61, 83, 120, 121, 124, 152
Christian electicism, 42
Christianity, 7, 27, 33, 34, 42, 47, 92, 107-108, 172
Christodoulidis, Sapphiros, 129
Christou, Panagiotis K., 175
Chrysostom, St. John, 60-61, 171, 174
Chrysostomos, Archimandrite, 174
Church Fathers, Eastern, 60, 66, 71, 72, 83, 103, 111, 114, 119, 121, 123, 124, 147, 155, 169, 174
Cicero, 3, 27, 173
clarity, 15, 23, 33, 38, 41, 57, 72, 77, 78, 84, 89, 90, 98, 104, 109, 116, 124, 143, 155
Clark University, 13, 33
classical philosophy, 13, 51-53, 166
classics, 15, 26, 53
Colgate University, 2, 9, 89
common sense, 20
compassion, 62
concentration, 31, 119
conciseness, 27, 57, 72, 87, 89, 98, 120, 124
Confession, 129

conscience, 36, 43, 169
Constantinople, 127, 135, 152
Copelston, Frederick C., 172
Cornford, F.M., 51
Cosmas Aitolos, St., 15, 94, 123, 126-129, 131, 155, 159, 165
cosmology, 49
courage, 38, 49, 61-62
creation, 43, 147
creativity, 61
Crusades, 99, 101

Damascene, St. John, 60-61, 113-114, 121, 123
Damascene, St. Peter, 119
Daniel, 123
David, 123
death, 123, 124, 129
de-Hellenization 107-108
de Magalhães-Vilhena, V., 172
democratic individual, 49
Democritos, 67
Demos, Raphael, 47, 163
Descartes, 62
destiny of man, *see* man
determinism, 60
Diognetos, 123
Dorotheos, Abba, 123
duty, 56

Eastern Church Fathers, *see* Church Fathers
ecclesiology, 174
eclecticism, Christian, 42
Ecumenical Patriarchate, 127, 135, 149, 152
"Ecumenism," 90, 99-101, 108

education, 42, 64-67, 81
  theory of, 14, 64-67, 167, 171
Edwards, Jonathan, 62
El Greco, 36, 104
Elias Ekdikos, 175
Emerson, Ralph Waldo, 23, 62
English philosophers, 51, 54
epistemology, 14, 21-22, 41, 53
ethics, 14, 38, 41, 42, 46, 47, 49, 54-57, 61, 65-67, 124, 135, 166, 171
Evagrios, 175
Evergetinos, 160
evil, 57, 62
existentialism, 60
existential orientation, 42
external world, 19-20, 46
Ezekiel, 123

faith, 29, 31, 34, 38, 61-62, 81, 105, 116, 119
Far East, 42
fasting, 84, 119, 129, 145, 147, 148
feelings, 36, 57, 61, 72, 123
filioque, 99
fine art, *see* art
forms, Aristotelian, 21; Platonic, 46
freedom, 49
free will, 29, 59-61, 62, 66
Fulbright Research Scholar, 2, 13, 23, 79, 83
future life, the, 121-124, 167

Gabriel of Dionysiou, 90

INDEX

God, 15, 16, 33, 34, 36, 43, 49, 57, 60, 62, 63, 72, 77, 83, 85, 90, 92, 105, 114, 116, 119-120, 129, 133, 142, 143, 147, 153, 155, 157, 160, 164, 170
good, the, 49, 60, 143, 157, 164
goodness, 56
goods (things good), 56-57
Gospels, 73, 78, 160
government, forms of, 49
Greco, El, 36
greed, 85
Greek letters, 15, 109-111, 166, 168
Greek Orthodox Church, 99-101
Greek Orthodox School of Theology, 13, 33, 79, 81
Gregory of Lesvos, 95
Gregory Palamas, St., 62, 121, 123
Gregory the Theologian, St., 121, 123, 171, 174
hagiography, 14
happiness, 62,
harmony, 46, 87
Harvard Universiy, 2, 7, 13, 19, 33, 47, 51, 55, 80, 163, 165
heart, 43, 101, 120, 147-148
Heidegger, Martin, 173
hell, 124
Hellenic College, 13, 170
hesychasm, 84, 145-147
history of philosophy, 14, 41

Hollins College, 143
Holy Cross Greek Orthodox School of Theology, 13, 33, 79, 81
Holy Mountain, see Athos,
Homer, 67
hope, 61-62, 147
humanism, 42-43
humility, 38, 61-62, 72, 116, 119, 129, 147, 152, 160
hymnody, 15, 36, 39, 75, 88, 89, 123, 124, 135, 170
Iakovos, Metropolitan of Mytilene, 94, 165
iconographers, Greek, 95, 98, 160, 174
iconography, 14-15, 16, 79, 83, 84, 95, 99, 112-116, 124, 166, 167-168, 170
icons, 35, 36, 98, 113-116, 159, 160, 167, 170
idealism, 20, 42
imagination, 43, 61, 66
immortality of the soul, 15, 27-31, 43, 49, 57, 61, 95-98, 123, 164
induction, 21
Inquisition, 99-101
Institute for Byzantine and Modern Greek Studies, 7, 13, 163-168
Institute of Balkan Studies at Thessaloniki, 79
intellect, 20-21
intuition, 19-21
inversion of life, 49
Isaiah the Solitary, 175
Isocrates, 67

Jakab, Irene, 170
James, William, 23, 25
John Chrysostom, St., 123
John Climacos, St., 62, 123, 160
John Damascene, St., 60-61, 113, 123, 170
justice, 38, 49, 62
Justin the Philosopher, 123

Kant, 21, 61
Karatzas, John, 65
Karmiris, Ioannis, 174
Kephalas, Nectarios, *see* Nectarios, St.
katharsis, 60, 105
Klein, Jacob, 173
knowledge, 19-22, 30, 31, 36, 38, 42, 47-49, 51, 53, 61, 104, 155, 170
Koidakis, Constantine, 95
Kollyvades Movement, 149
Kontoglou, Fotis (Photios), 29, 59, 61-62, 73-78, 84, 87, 103-105, 113, 114, 163, 164, 167, 168, 171
Kopsidis, Rallis, 84, 87

language, 13, 66, 79, 81, 111
Lesvos, 15, 29, 60, 65-67, 93-98, 104, 165
Lewis, Clarence Irving, 163
Locke, John, 60
logic, 14, 41, 66
Lossky, Vladimir, 113-114, 173
Louvaris, Nicholas, 42-43
love, 38, 60, 61, 90, 92, 116, 119, 120, 129, 147, 152, 155, 160, 169, 171

Macarios of Corinth, St., 15, 127, 130-133, 165, 175
Macarios the Egyptian, St., 121, 123
Maguire, Henry, 174
man, 19, 23-26, 30-31, 43, 46, 47-50, 66, 77, 123, 124, 160, 164, 165
  nature and destiny of, 15, 43, 46-50, 59, 124
Marangoulas, Michael, 166
Mark of Ephesus, St., 168
Mark the Ascetic, St., 123, 175
martyrs, 133, 139
materialism, 105, 147
material world, 19-20, 42, 60, 114
mathematics, 60, 65, 66, 172
matter, 19-20
Maximos the Confessor, St., 60-61
McTaggart, J.E., 51
medieval Western philosophers, 14, 42, 172
meditation, 119, 157
meekness, 62, 116
memory, 66, 123
mental practices, 119, 145
mentalism ("idealism"), 20
metaphysics, 14, 19-22, 41, 51-53, 60, 65, 95, 124, 166, 169
Michelis, P.A., 59, 62-63, 171, 172-173
mind, 20, 61
modern European philosophy, 14, 47, 60, 63

INDEX

modern Greek civilization, 13, 104, 171
modern Greek literature, 169
modern Greek philosophy, 14, 27-31, 59-63, 164
modern Greek studies, 89
modern Greek thought, 13, 14, 27-31, 33, 40-43, 64-67, 164, 168, 171
modernization, 107-108, 165
monasticism, 83-94, 131, 145-148, 159-160, 164, 165, 175
Moore, G.E., 14, 54-57, 166
morality, 46
Motovilov, Nicholas, 143, 147
Moutsopoulos, E., 173
Moutsopoulos, Nicholas, 87
music, 34, 36, 46, 66, 79, 83, 84, 88, 89
mysticism, 77, 84, 133, 143, 147, 155

Nectarios of Aegina, St., 15, 29, 99, 123, 127, 153-157, 167
Neilos the Ascetic, St., 175
Nicodemos the Hagiorite, St., 15, 99, 119, 120, 123, 127, 134-138, 155, 165, 168, 171, 175
Nikephoros of Chios, St., 15, 139-142, 149, 166
Nikephoros Theotokis, 43
Niketas Stethatos, 62, 123
novelists, 41

obedience, 152, 160
oligarchic individual, 49

orderliness, 49, 66, 85, 89
organic unities, principle of, 57
Orthodox saints, 126-161
Orthodoxy, 7, 15, 27, 31, 33, 34, 36, 39, 43, 60, 63, 66-67, 73-75, 77, 78, 79-81, 89, 95, 103-116, 121-160, 164, 166, 167, 168-171, 174-175
Ouspensky, Leonide, 113, 114

painting, 46, 84
Palmer, G.E.H., 175
Panselinos, Manuel, 36, 104
Papanikolaou, Vasilios, 159, 160
Papanoutsos, E.P., 171, 172
Paradise, 124, 137
Parios, Athanasios, 99, 123, 131
passionlessness, 116
patience, 119, 147
Patristics, 37, 67, 107
Paul the Apostle, 83, 111, 121, 123, 174
peace of the soul, 147, 152, 157
perception, 19-22, 120, 123
personalism, 42
personality, 31, 42
Peter the Apostle, 121
Petros the Peloponnesian, 72
Philemon, Abba, 175
Philokalia, 36, 131, 133, 147, 160, 170, 175
philosophic wonder, 47, 49

philosophy, 7, 14, 17-67, 84, 98, 111, 155, 163-173
philosophy of education, 15, 41-42
philosophy of history, 41-42
philosophy of religion, 14, 42
philosophy of science, 41-42
Philotheos the Sinaite, 175
physical world, *see* material world
piety, 61-62
Piompinos, Phoivos, 174
Plato, 14, 44-50, 51-53, 56, 57, 60, 61, 62, 67, 165, 166, 169, 170, 171, 172, 173
Plomarion, 93-94
Plotinos, 62
Plutarch, 67
poetry, 41, 46, 66, 111, 139, 155, 170
political philosophy, 14, 41-42
prayer, 83, 84, 85, 92, 119-120, 137, 143, 145, 147, 160
preciseness, 57, 98, 109
Pre-Socratic philosophers, 14
prudence, 62
psychology, 14, 49, 61
"pure memory," 19-21
"pure perception," 19-20
purification, 36, 38, 60, 92, 105, 119
purity, 90, 119

rational insight, 19
rational man, the, 168
rationalism, 60

Read, Herbert, 172
reality, 19-22, 36, 38, 49, 53
reason, 21, 43, 46, 49, 66, 168, 169
relations, 51-53, 55, 166
religion, 7, 15, 42, 47, 61, 63, 111, 114, 124, 173
repentance, 92, 119
responsibility, 49, 59-60
resurrection, 43, 123, 124
Rexine, John E., 2, 27, 173, 174
rhetoric, 46, 111, 174
Ross, W.D., 55, 56
Russell, Bertrand, 51
Russian iconography, 75, 113
Russian spirituality, 143-148

sainthood, 117, 166, 170
saints, 7, 89, 90, 94, 104, 117-120, 127-161, 165-167
salvation, 62, 116
Santayana, 51
Sardelis, Kostas, 127
Sarou, Emily, 139
Savvas the New, St., 15, 158-161, 167
science, 21, 29, 41, 42, 60, 65-66, 123, 168
  critique of, 40, 42-43
  philosophy of, 42
scientific knowledge, 42
scientific materialism, 42
scientism, 42-43
Scripture, Holy, 67, 71, 94, 107, 109-111, 119, 121, 123, 124, 129
sculpture, 46, 99

Index

secularism, 85, 90, 92, 94, 101, 104-105, 107
self-concentration, 31, 90
self-knowledge, 49
self-perfection, 36, 72, 87
Seraphim of Sarov, St., 15, 120, 127, 143-148, 149, 167
Serbia, 127, 164
Sheldon Traveling Fellowship, 55
Sherrard, Philip, 175
silence, 119, 145, 147, 148
simplicity, 33, 38, 61-62, 71, 77, 85, 87, 104, 129
sincerity, 85, 90
Skaltsounis, Ioannis, 29
smoking, 168
social philosophy, 41-42
Socrates, 30, 172
solitude, 84, 92, 148
Solomon, 121
Sophocles, 67
soul, 27-31, 36, 43, 47-49, 57, 59-61, 63, 77, 85, 95, 105, 120, 121, 123, 124, 147, 164, 165, 170
Spetsieris, Joachim, 155
spirit, 20
spiritual knowledge, 105
spirituality, 38, 94, 116, 127, 129, 137, 138, 139, 142, 157, 175
spiritual world, 114
structure, 21-22, 49
subjectivism, 20, 21
Symeon of Thessaloniki, 175
Synods, Ecumenical, 107, 109-111, 113-114
synthesis, 22, 66
Tatakis, Basil N., 173
temperance, 49, 62
Terzakis, Angelos, 174
Theocletos of Dionysiou, 92, 94
Theodorakopoulos, I.N., 29-31, 59, 61, 171
Theodore of Edessa, St., 62, 175
theology, 13, 15, 33, 34, 38, 41, 49, 81, 95, 98, 104, 111, 113, 116, 135, 155, 170
Theophilos Hatzimichael, 104
theosis, 43, 60, 116, 119, 120, 142, 147
Theotokis, Nikephoros, 43
Theotokos, 145-147
therapy, 170
Thessaloniki, 79
Three Great Hierarchs, the, 171, 174
Thomism, 14, 51-53, 166
Thucydides, 67
timocratic individual, 49
Topalis, Basil, 95
tradition, 103-105, 107-108, 119, 133, 135, 145, 165, 169
tragedy, 46
transcendentalism, 36, 38, 42
Trubetskoi, Eugene N., 113-114
truth, 34, 36, 38, 44, 46, 49, 105, 120, 147
Tufts University, 13
tyrannic individual, 49

union of the Churches, 99-101, 164
United States, see America
unity of the Church, 174
universals, 21
universe, 23-26, 49
University of Athens, 13, 23, 33, 83
University of North Carolina, 13, 33, 80

values,
  spiritual, 29, 31, 87
  world of, 42
virginity, 129
virtue, 36, 38, 43, 49, 59, 60, 66, 116, 119, 135, 142, 147, 152
Vrailas-Armenis, Petros, 29, 59, 173

Ware, Kallistos, 175
ways of sanctity, 117-120

Wellesley College, 13
Wheaton College, 13, 33
Whitehead, A.N., 23, 51, 62
Whitman, Cedric H., 174
Wild, John D., 19, 47, 163
will, 43, 61
wisdom, 34, 43, 46, 49, 147
women, 129
World Council of Churches, 108
worhip, 36

Xenophon, 67

Yale University, 89
Yugoslavia, 77

Zachariou, Fotis, 87
Zeldin, Mary-Barbara, 143, 144, 147, 167
Zervakos, Philotheos, 149, 152
Zolotas, George I., 139